Jean Cocteau
The Art of Cinema

Jean Cocteau
The Art of Cinema

Compiled and edited by
André Bernard and Claude Gauteur

Translated from the French by
Robin Buss

With introductory essays by
Robin Buss, André Bernard and Claude Gauteur

Marion Boyars
London · New York

Published in paperback in 1994

Published in hardcover in Great Britain and the United States
in 1992 by Marion Boyars Publishers
24 Lacy Road London SW15 1NL
237 East 39th Street New York, NY 10016

Distributed in Australia and New Zealand by Peribo Pty Ltd, Terrey Hills, NSW

Originally published in 1988 by Editions Belfond, Paris, under the title *Du
Cinématographe*
© by Editions Belfond, 1988
© This translation Marion Boyars Publishers, 1992

British Library Cataloguing-in-Publication Data
Cocteau, Jean, *1889–1963*
    The art of cinema
    I. Title   II. Bernard, André III. Gauteur, Claude
    791.43

Library of Congress Cataloging in Publication Data
Cocteau, Jean, 1889–1963.
    [Cinématographe.   English]
    The art of cinema/compiled and edited by André Bernard and
Claude Gauteur; translated from the French by Robin Buss; with
introductory essays by Robin Buss, André Bernard, and Claude
Gauteur.
    Translation of: Du cinématographe.
    Includes bibliographical references and index.
    1. Motion pictures.   I. Bernard, André, 1934–.   II. Gauteur,
Claude, 1935–.   III. Title.
PN1994.C53813   1992
791.43—dc20   91–43546

ISBN 0–7145–2947–8 hardcover
ISBN 0–7145–2974–5 paperback

Typeset in Baskerville 11 on 13 pt and Futura book by
Ann Buchan (Typesetters), Shepperton
Printed and bound in Great Britain by
Itchen Printers Ltd, Southampton

Design by Susi Mawani
Cover photograph: Still from The Blood of a Poet by Raymond Rohaner

Contents

III *Poésie de Cinéma* / 131

IV Unpublished Synopses / 195

Filmography / 217

Bibliography / 220

Index / 221

Introduction
by *Robin Buss*

Jean Cocteau (1889-1963) was born a few years before the invention of moving pictures, and died a few years after the start of the French New Wave. In this collection of writings, he recalls as a child seeing the first Lumière Brothers' films and expresses his delight, as an old man, in François Truffaut's *Les Quatre cents coups* and *Jules et Jim*. Although not very studious, or at all academic, he was a precocious adolescent who founded a literary review and read his first poems in public, at the Théâtre Femina, when he was only 17, mixing with most of the well-known writers, painters and musicians in Paris and managing to be involved, at least marginally, in all the main cultural movements and scandals of the time. He was a figure in the avant-garde, made still more aware of belonging to the new machine age by his experiences as an ambulance driver in the First World War, and he could hardly ignore the existence of cinema.

There were peculiar reasons, however, for his lifelong enthusiasm. Cocteau had the talents of a polymath and the instincts of a dilettante. He drew, painted, wrote, composed: poems, plays, novels, essays, songs, sketches, murals. He worked quickly, in flashes of brilliance, catching the inspiration, open to everything that was going on around him. His novel *Les Enfants terribles* (1929), written in three weeks during a cure for opium addiction, refers directly or obliquely to American evangelism, to Isadora Duncan, to Coco Chanel, to *Macbeth*, to film stars, to Nietzsche, to Racine and other writers, French or foreign, to Egyptian religion, and much more, all these references being in some way suggestive and illuminating, lightly folded into a soufflé which the consumer can swallow without noticing the calories. This was Cocteau's method: the affectation of dandyism that conceals hard work. What brought all these activities together, and ensured the integrity of the artist behind the pretence of superficiality, was what Cocteau called 'poetry'.

By poetry, he did not mean verse. The notion of poetry that allowed him to classify all his works under this heading (*'Poésie de Roman'* for the novels, *'Poésie critique'* for the essays and *'Poésie de cinéma'* for the films) derived from the ideology of Romanticism. Poetry was not related to a particular literary form, but a quality that could be present in prose, in music, in landscape or even in the lifestyle of Cocteau's *Enfants terribles*. But for Cocteau, unlike the Romantics, it was not some vague essence, but a process or mechanism, inherent in things (including the most everyday objects) that, once released, would operate mysteriously on the mind. The role of the artist, the poet, is to evoke the Poetry — hence the frequent references to magic and the Muses — and to create the conditions in which it could work: 'the poetry *functions* better in the garage', he says here, about his film *L'Eternel retour*, scorning those critics who had found the lovers' castle more 'poetic'.

He scorns them because he scorns their limited concept of poetry. Poetry did not just hang around in picturesque places with a select gang of 'poetic' subjects, it was everywhere for the poet to uncover. Human fate was determined by the mechanisms that could be perceived through its mysterious charm. The task was, therefore, an essentially practical one: that of a craftsman, though not necessarily in verse, who allows it to function. And when the poet Cocteau chose to operate through film, he repeatedly compares himself to someone making a table, whose concern is solely to ensure that the structure is solid, the drawers run smoothly and the legs stand firm. The audience will then come, like mediums to a seance, lay their hands on the table and see if they can conjure up spirits by making it 'turn'.

Not only was cinema, therefore, a perfectly proper

medium for the poet, but it might also be an especially fruitful one. For one thing, Cocteau asserts that the underlying mechanism of cinema is like that of dreams. He is deeply suspicious of intellectuals and rationalists, feeling that dreamers and children are far more susceptible to poetry. Secondly, while it creates a hypnotic state in its audience, watching a film is also like the experience of dreaming because of its 'realism': we 'believe' what we see, even when reason tells us it is impossible, and because the mechanics of film production allow much greater and more convincing use of special effects than those of the theatre, the film-maker can make 'real' the unreal figments of the imagination.

The films that a poet makes will be of a certain kind — probably not, for example, films meant purely for commercial and exploitative ends, or propaganda. But neither will they, according to Cocteau's idea of poetry, be films that are deliberately 'poetic'. He disliked the élitism of 'art cinema' and his writings on cinema show evidence of an eclectic taste: *Ben-Hur, Pépé-le-Moko, Battleship Potemkin, Monsieur Verdoux, Le Sang des bêtes, Les Yeux sans visage* — comedies, melodrama, *films noirs*, documentaries, horror. Just as poetry 'functions' better in a garage than in a castle, so it may be found in the inventive gags of slapstick comedy, if anything more easily than in a self-consciously tragic work of art. Cocteau enjoyed 'popular' entertainment, and his own screenplays (see, for example, the outlines in the last section of this book) often draw on melodrama and vaudeville. The pleasure he takes in melodramatic storylines, which have the poignancy of popular melodies, sordid backstreets and garish bars, is parallelled in his love of special effects, particularly the kind that involve changing one object into another. The metamorphosis of a wallet into a flower (the final image in his last film, *Le Testament d'Orphée*) is, for Cocteau, potentially as poetic an idea as the legendary metamorphoses in classical myth.

He also knew, and wrote with affection, about film directors and actors: Chaplin, Welles, Bresson, Marlene Dietrich. He met Chaplin in 1936, on an 80-day round-the-

world journey in the footsteps of Jules Verne's hero, under-
taken after a bet with *France-Soir*. We see him with Welles in
a hotel lobby in Venice at the time of the Festival and find
him paying tribute to Gérard Philipe and Jacques Becker
after their deaths. He was closest of all to the actors and
film-makers with whom he worked, the closest of these, of
course, being his companion Jean Marais.

Cocteau's first film, *Le Sang d'un poète* (1930), is also the
most recognizably an 'art movie'. Although made five years
after his open breach with the Surrealists, it clearly belongs
to the period of experimental film-making in France during
the 1920s which produced Buñuel's *L'Age d'or* (also financed
by the Comte de Noailles). It is a compendium of Cocteau's
themes, containing references to the Orpheus myth and to
the snowball fight from *Les Enfants terribles*. Most important
of all, it allowed Cocteau to explore the potential of the
medium and the effects that he was to use in a more
disciplined way in later works.

After *Le Sang d'un poète*, he did not make another film until
La Belle et la Bête (1946), an experience that he recorded in *La
Belle et la Bête: Journal d'un film* (1946; Eng. trs., *Diary of a
Film*, 1950). What the diary records is a succession of
experiences so gruesome that it is surprising its author ever
again wanted to see the inside of a cinema studio: not only
are there the usual technical problems, but Marais has boils
and unending problems with his make-up, while Cocteau
himself endures a whole catalogue of diseases (principally
shingles and exhaustion) on top of the ordinary traumas of
directing. Incredibly, this was the start of a period of
sustained work for the cinema, continuing with *L'Aigle à deux
têtes* (1947) and *Les Parents terribles* (1948), and ending with
his undoubted masterpiece, *Orphée* (1950). After that, he was
to make one more film, *Le Testament d'Orphée* (1959), in which
he acts the main role.

What is most remarkable about Cocteau's films is their
consistency with the rest of his work and fidelity to his
personal obsessions — something that was only possible
because of the understanding of his team. He pays frequent

tribute to them here: Georges Auric, who wrote the music for every film except the last; Christian Bérard, art director on *La Belle et la Bête*, *L'Aigle à deux têtes* and *Les Parents terribles*; the designer Georges Wakhévitch (*L'Aigle à deux têtes*); and the photographers Henri Alekan (*La Belle et la Bête*) and Michel Kelber (*Les Parents terribles*). As well as being ahead of his time in realizing the role of the audience in 'making' a work of art, he readily acknowledged that cinema is a cooperative venture in which the author-director can only succeed thanks to the efforts of others. Few directors have been as generous in their praise for their assistants, yet there can be few filmographies that so clearly represent the work of an *auteur* as Cocteau's.

He attached enormous importance to friendship and says so often: the heart invariably presides over the intellect. This means, on the one hand, that his writing on film contains little in the way of theoretical speculation, apart from developing his concepts of poetry, which he does in his own terms (table-making, the Muse of Cinema, etc.), and virtu-ally no hostile criticism. If he dislikes a film, he prefers to ignore it. When he talks about his friends, he does so in order to praise them and to direct attention to the excellence of their work. In some cases (for example, his fulsome attempt to express the magic of Marlene Dietrich), he is in a situation where convention demands this sort of thing: he would hardly agree to come on stage and introduce Marlene if he had anything disparaging to say about her. But, frequently, affection persuades him to behave as if he were under the same kind of obligation, when he is not.

The result is that, as criticism, these writings may seem bland. But the absence of malice is, at worst, an attractive fault; and all the more so in a man who had himself been subjected to some virulent personal criticism. Reviewing Jean Delannoy's film, *L'Eternel retour*, for which Cocteau wrote the script, the critic François Vinneuil, in the Fascist newspaper *Je Suis Partout* (October 1943) described Cocteau as 'an aged weathercock of the third sex' who 'in his female capriciousness' followed every fashion, 'a bedraggled clown', 'a frenzied coquette' and a 'perpetually inverted intelligence'. This is certainly not bland, but neither is it in any way appealing. Apart from the pointed reference to Cocteau's homosexuality, the accusation of time-serving is grossly unfair, and particularly rich from a contributor to a collaborationist paper.

The other difficulty with any anthology of such occasional writings is that it may become repetitious. This is inevitable in a book that was never designed to be one: what is collected here are notes, essays and journalism originally designed for a variety of readers and places. Some show evidence of having been written in haste, and in others concepts, comparisons or quotations that pleased Cocteau are repeated, occasionally word for word. His dandyism did not extend to the nicety of refusing to re-use a good line to a new audience, and it is only because all those audiences have become the single readership of this book, that he can occasionaly be seen to be telling the same story over and over.

Despite that, this is a fascinating collection. For a start, it illuminates Cocteau's own work for the cinema, with detailed discussions of his aims in *La Belle et la Bête*, an outline for the scenario of *Orphée*, responses to criticisms of *Le Testament d'Orphée*, reflections on the relationship between cinema and theatre and an explanation of his contrary intentions in making *L'Aigle à deux têtes* and *Les Parents terribles*. The final section of unpublished synopses reveals a good deal about Cocteau's use of elements from melodrama and his belief in the 'mechanisms' of fate: the luckless crook who wants to be caught, the couple who exchange temperaments because of hypnotism or a blow on the head.

Most of all, it shows him as a militant in the cause of the Seventh Art. He disliked the word 'cinema', preferring to use the already obsolete term *cinématographe*, which I have translated 'cinematography'. *Cinématographe*, also the name given by the Lumière Brothers to their camera, became Cocteau's property in the alternative sense: the Petit Robert dictionary describes it as 'obsolete or didactic', supplies the single definition 'cinema' and illustrates it with the following quotation from Cocteau: 'Cinematography is an art. It will liberate itself from industrial slavery.'

This is splendidly concise. What Cocteau hoped to do, was to revive the term, intending to distinguish the art of 'cinematography' from the ephemeral entertainment supplied by 'cinema'. He wanted to breathe life into the dead word, just as he tried (in his poetry, his plays, his films and his criticism) to give modern meanings to classical myths: the Muse of Cinema, he tells us, is impatient; she will not give a work of cinematography time to establish itself, as poetry (verse poetry) is able to do. In more everyday terms: it costs very little to publish a book of poetry, but huge sums are involved in making a film, so the people who finance it want to see a return on their investment, and preferably before the next century. So the art of cinema is in thrall to its backers, who favour the subjects which they know will attract an immediate audience.

This over-hasty cinema industry is typified by Hollywood. Cocteau was not inspired by facile anti-Americanism: he shows his enthusiasm in these pages for Welles, Vidor, Chaplin and De Mille, as well as for much more obscure figures, like Robert Montgomery. He does feel that the postwar fashion in Europe for, say, American pulp fiction and Westerns, is misjudged, and he writes occasionally about the influence here of the Hollywood star system, for example in his perceptive pieces on Brigitte Bardot and James Dean. But his aim, as usual, is not to undermine, but to open up: to create parallel routes through which young people can get into making films and find audiences. He actively supported the Festival du Cinéma Maudit in Biarritz and he expounds at length on the virtues of 16mm film, calling it *le grand seize* — 'great 16': he was wrong in his belief that the future of independent cinema lay in this format, but right to promote the virtues of independence. He is equally right in his understanding that the cinema 'audience' is, in fact, several audiences, and that ways must be found to reach them, to preserve films from the past and to give new films time to work.

As often, his positions on these things are adopted with an awareness that suggests an element of self-dramatization: I am on the side of the young, he says, on the side of art against Mammon, in the dock with the accused, never on the bench with the judges. 'When the public reproaches you with something, cultivate it — it is you,' was one of his favourite maxims. False modesty was not one of his faults, and he quotes, with satisfaction, one or two kind things that have been said about his work. Having chosen to place himself in the dock, he adjures criticism, and his repeated claim that he was not really a film-maker, combined with his anti-intellectual stance, means that he is not a cinema theorist either.

Yet his writings on cinema are an absorbing testimony from one of the most individualistic of French directors, who was consistent in his promotion of a particular idea of cinema as art — distinct from what is usually known as 'art cinema'. They are indispensible for a complete understanding of his own films and will remain valuable for the insights they give into the medium itself, at a particular moment in its history. Despite an appearance of dilettantism, Cocteau was never a dilettante: he approached his work for the cinema with intense conviction. The films themselves remain the most persuasive tribute to his lifelong passion for 'cinematography', and this collection, though Cocteau never intended these disparate pieces to form one, uncovers the mechanism by which that passion operates, in a way that he would have entirely approved.

Preface to the Second Edition
by *André Bernard and Claude Gauteur*

Du Cinématographe was first published in France in the Autumn of 1973, on the tenth anniversary of Jean Cocteau's death. Since then, it has become almost unobtainable. This second edition is enlarged and enriched by the addition of several texts which we had previously missed, but later managed to uncover.

Cocteau liked to describe himself as 'a phoney-director' — saying that 'cinematography' was not his profession and that he made use of film as a medium which allowed him to show what poetry, novels, theatre and essays could merely describe. 'I have nothing to do with cinema,' he stated in 1923, 'because I have directed my energies elsewhere, and I should have to devote myself exclusively to it.'[1] In fact, he made his first film in 1930 and his last in 1960. Between the two, there were periods of inactivity amounting to almost two decades, and an active period of ten years (1942-1952).

Thirty years on, he would protest that André Gide 'claimed I took advantage of changing fashions, while on the contrary I fought against all of them, either through books, or in the theatre, or on film. In reality, all I did was to turn my lamp this way and that, to illuminate various facets of the themes that obsess me: the loneliness of individuals, waking dreams and childhood, that dreadful state of childhood from which I shall never escape.'[2]

---

1   To Frédéric Lefèvre, *Les Nouvelles littéraires*, March 24, 1923.
2   To Gabriel d'Aubarède, *Les Nouvelles littéraires*, Feb. 12, 1953. Despite this, Gide

He was constantly to reaffirm this thematic and aesthetic creed. Already, in 1925, the future director of *La Belle et la Bête* and future adaptor of *La Princesse de Clèves* (which he had once hoped to direct himself), was writing in *Le Secret professionnel*:

> Nothing is more disturbing than aristocracy, of whatever kind. In the social hierarchy, a book like *La Princesse de Clèves* is a masterpiece of the genre. This divine, human and inhuman fairy story sheds a terrible vulgarity on novels which depict what Tolstoy calls 'the upper reaches'. Beside Mme de Lafayette's novel, the world of the best novels partakes of the underworld.[3]

In the same book, the future Baron Fantôme and future director of *Orphée* and *Le Testament d'Orphée* gave us this image:

> The poet is like the dead in the sense that he walks invisibly among the living and is only imprecisely seen by them after his death; that is to say, in the case of the dead, when they appear in the form of ghosts.[4]

Thomas l'Imposteur inspired the following comparison:

> Cinematography ought to develop psychology without a text. In *Thomas*, I have tried to develop a text without psychology, or at least one so rudimentary that it is comparable to the few explanatory lines of a model film. Analysis in the bare pseudo-novel and the landscapes of the pseudo-descriptive novel are equivalent to one another.[5]

Describing Picasso's sets for Stravinsky's *Pulcinella*, he also

---

would have liked Cocteau to direct *Isabelle* (see *Journal d'un inconnu*, Grasset, 1953, p.113)

3   *Le Secret professionnel*, Au Sans-Pareil, 1925, p. 2. Reprinted in *Le Rappel à l'ordre*, Stock, 1926, pp. 177-178. In *Le Grand écart*, Mme Bernard already compares her love for Jacques to 'that of the Duc de Nemours and the Princesse de Clèves'.

4   *Ibid.*, p. 89 and p. 252.

5   *Les Nouvelles littéraires*, Oct. 27, 1923. Reprinted in *Le Rappel à l'ordre*, p. 265.

(as yet unwittingly) described the caravan in *Les Parents terribles*, spied on by the indiscreet lens of the camera:

> Remember the mysteries of childhood, the landscapes children secretly discover in a blot, the views of Vesuvius at night in the stereoscope, chimneys at Christmas and *rooms seen through a keyhole*, and you will understand the spirit of these sets which fill the stage at the Opera with no other contrivance than grey canvasses and a house for performing dogs.[6]

Look at *Portraits-Souvenir*. Here, 'the intimate surroundings of Edouard de Max' suggest 'the domestic interior of a gypsy caravan'. Elsewhere, an Austrian archduke exclaims, of an eagle brought down by a huntsman: 'What! Has it only got one head?' And yet again, the Comtesse de Noailles looks like 'Minerva, her forehead resting on her lance. Stiff, leaning forward, helmeted, like the figure seven, she meditates.'[7] *Les Parents terribles*, *L'Aigle à deux têtes*, *Le Testament d'Orphée* . . .

Finally, in *Journal d'un inconnu*, this confession:

> The power of flowing blood is peculiar. You feel that the lava of your inner fire is trying to recognize itself in it. I am disgusted by the sight of blood, yet I entitled a film 'The Blood of a Poet' — *Le Sang d'un poète*; I show blood in it several times and the theme of Oedipus, which I have used repeatedly, is drenched in blood.[8]

This is, moreover, a reminder that Jean Cocteau was already a film-maker even before he directed his first scene. According to Henri Langlois, 'Cocteau and the cinema met in childhood', Melies coming before Minerva and opening the mirror for him: 'The cinema did not wait until *Le Sang d'un poète* before entering Cocteau's work. It is everywhere in *Le*

---

6 'Picasso' in *Le Rappel à l'ordre*, p. 288. Emphasis added.
7 *Portraits-Souvenir*, Grasset, 1935, pp. 155, 217 and 218 respectively.
8 *Journal d'un inconnu*, p. 178

Cap de Bonne-Espérance, it found its way into the poetry of *Plain-Chant* and it is in *Opéra*.'[9]. And also in *Le Grand écart* — which, unlike *Les Enfants terribles* and *Thomas l'imposteur*, has surprisingly not yet appealed to any film-maker. Admittedly, the first lines of the novel do not seem particularly favourable to the new art which Canudo baptised the Seventh ('Jacques Forestier wept easily. Cinematography, bad music and popular stories reduced him to tears', 'false tokens of the heart' which he hid 'in the darkness of a theatre box or alone with a book', as opposed to tears that are 'deep', 'true' or 'rare'). But, in reality, the young novelist literally cuts, directs, edits and mixes his story.

Take, for example, this passage from wide-angle shot to closeup: 'As quickly as a woman — a small figure in a group on the cinema screen — is followed by the face of the same woman in the foreground, six times lifesize', and throwing everything into darkness around it. Or, again, this exchange of magnetic looks, in which eroticism and narcissism alternate:

> This time, desire encountered a sensitive surface and Germaine's response was the very image of Jacques, in the same way that the screen delivers the film which, unless it met some obstacle, would only blossom in whiteness. Jacques saw his own image in this desire and, for the first time, was overwhelmed by meeting himself: he loved himself in Germaine.

Elsewhere, sound and colour reinforce distortions of the image and special effects:

> Jacques looks at the track. It lengthens and bends in the distorting mirrors. The music also changes, as when one amuses oneself while listening to an orchestra, by blocking and unblocking one's ears. He sees Peter and Germaine, monks by El Greco. They stretch, go green,

9   *Cahiers Jean Cocteau*, N° 3, Gallimard, 1972, pp. 28 and 30.

rise heavenwards, enraptured, thunderstruck by the mercury lamps. Then they roll, far, far away: a broad, dwarfish Germaine and Stopwell becoming a Louis-Philippe chair with its feet kicking to left and right. The bar heaves. Louise thrusts forward a blurred face from an artistic film. Her mouth is moving and Jacques cannot hear a word.

A little further on, deep focus shots are followed by narrow focus shots, superimpositions (or jump cuts) and travelling shots:

Louise, with the same movement of her chin . . . indicated the unfortunate man to Germaine.

'He will get over it,' she said.

The remark was humane in the sense that the law considers merciful the bullet fired by an officer at pointblank range into an executed man who is still breathing.

'A cigarette?' Stopwell offered.

Charmingly considerate, the execution squad.

. . . in Germaine's car. Jacques, hoisted up, lolling around, with no strength left, observed a blurred landscape on both sides. A profile: Mahieddine, the Odéon, posters, the Luxembourg gardens, the Gambrinus inn, the fountain. Stopwell was being driven back.[10]

Everything is a snapshot, including the image that pursues the hero, of his two friends asleep after making love, 'laced together like initials', the 'queen of hearts without her dress', the 'many-limbed Hindu idol'. They might be covered with that 'foam of lace and chiffon' which the poet has also provided, still remaining resolutely unfashionable.

What was the source of his passion for cinema?, *L'Ecran français* asked him in 1946: 'A William Hart film . . . , *The*

---

10   *Le Grand écart*, Stock, 1923, pp. 52–53, 58, 147–148 and 150–151 respectively.

Cheat with Sessue Hayakawa ... , Chaplin's films'[11].
Indeed, as early as 1919, given free rein to write about
anything in the newspaper *Paris-Midi*, Jean Cocteau advised
his readers to see *Shoulder Arms* and *Carmen of the Klondyke* ('a
lost film . . . the beauty of which survives only through him',
Langlois points out) and expressed his wish to see 'the new
medium at the service of a new art form': 'Until that happy
day arrives, make do with what we have and seek out the
best.'[12]

Need one mention that he was to find the best and to share
his discoveries from one book to another. In *Opium* (1930), he
highlights 'three great films': Buster Keaton's *Sherlock Junior*,
Chaplin's *Gold Rush* and Eisenstein's *Battleship Potemkin*,
adding, as soon as he had seen them, Luis Buñuel's *Un chien
andalou* and *L'Age d'or*. He expresses his admiration for
Harpo Marx and Ernst Lubitsch in a few lines, in *Essai de
critique indirecte* (1932); and, over several pages in *Mon premier
voyage* (1937), his admiration for Charlie Chaplin, also
recording a visit to King Vidor while he was passing through
Hollywood. *Le Foyer des artistes* (1947), a selection of his
articles in *Ce soir* and *Comoedia*, gives a favourable mention to
Modern Times, *Tarzan Escapes*, *Les Anges du péché*, Greta Garbo
in *Anna Karenina* and *Camille*, and Arletty in *Madame Sans-
Gêne*.

This was the tip of the iceberg. What was hidden were the
many writings about film-making, articles, prefaces, tributes
and notes, which remained scattered or unpublished, and
which the death of the author, an active member of the Club
des Amis du Septième Art and Objectif 49, honorary presi-
dent of the jury of the Cannes Festival and of the Fédération
Française des Ciné-Clubs, prevented him from collecting
and prefacing himself. This is another 'professional secret',
another 'diary of an unknown man': Cocteau as a film writer.

---

11   *L'Ecran français*, N° 68, Oct. 16, 1946.
12   *Paris-Midi*, April 28, 1919. Reprinted in *Carte blanche*, *La Sirène*, 1920, then in *Le
Rappel à l'ordre*.

Jean Cocteau was suspicious of 'cinematographic work', even though it brought him the joys of exercising a craft and of working in a team, 'because the hypnosis it induces in us is such that it becomes hard to tell where it ends. Even when the film breaks away and, having devoured us, revolves with a casual and detached life of its own, more distant than that of the stars, the machine in us is still subject to it and will not be wiped clean.'[13]

The lasting effects of this hypnosis are proved both by his writings about his own films, and by his writings on the poetry of cinema, the cinema of poetry, film-makers, films and actors whom he liked and whom he liked to like. Those who love his work will find him here, loyal to his principles and to himself: a cabinet-maker, not a medium; suffering from the difficulty of being and creating; always in the dock with the accused, never on the bench with the judges.

---

13   *La Difficulté d'être* Paris, Paul Morihien, 1947, p. 157.

Translator's note

In this translation, film titles are given in the original language, when this is French, English/American or German; otherwise in English. Apart from Cocteau's own films, most are easily identifiable from the text, or very well-known. When I feel this may not be the case, I have added the director's name and the date of the film in square brackets after the title. Obviously, since these are occasional pieces, they contain a lot of passing references to writers, directors, artists and other personalities. Most of these are so familiar as not to need annotation (e.g. Picasso); so casually cited that a footnote would seem pedantic (e.g. Marie Bashkirtseff); or easily placed from the context. I have, therefore, kept explanatory notes, both outside and inside the text, to a minimum.

'FILM, the new muse.'
(*Poésie*, 1920)

'My next work will be a film.'
(*Opium*, 1930)

'You're right, here I am again. One never finishes saying goodbye.'
(Post-scriptum to *Testament d'Orphée*, 1960.)

1 Cinematography and Poetry

I am altogether opposed to popular entertainment because I consider that all good entertainment is popular. The proof is to be found in cinematography which extends beyond the theatre-going audience. A mass audience is without preconceptions. It never forms a judgement based on the author or the actors. *It believes in them.* This is the childhood audience — and the best.

A film, conceived without any moral or social ideas, but with passion, is liable to be deformed in the distorting mirror of its first-run audience. When it moves into general release, it can breathe, walk, live. Our role is to construct a firm table, not to make it turn. A carpenter cannot be a medium, or vice versa. The collective hypnosis into which the cinema audience is plunged by light and shade is very like a spiritualist seance. Then, the film expresses something other than what it is, something that no one can predict. In any event, the measure of love with which it is charged will affect the masses more than any subtle and witty concoction.

To sum up: I know of no élite and no tribunal which can take upon itself to judge what a film will unleash in its immeasurable course. The only jurisdiction to which a film should be subject concerns its style and its expressive power. The rest is a mystery and will always remain so.
[Speech at the Institut des Hautes Etudes Cinématographiques, September 9, 1946].

Theatre and Cinema

I think we can say that the theatre will emerge from the long restorative sleep into which it was plunged by the shock of cinematography. The mind has already started to weary of a succession of flat images continuously unreeling on the old magic lantern screen and displaying the cross-section of a ghostly world which, with the discovery of depth in noise and sound (minus, I might add, the element of shock), has been deprived of much of its charm.

Do not be misled, however; this charm has been replaced by another, peculiar charm that derives from a feeling of unease, a disequilibrium, a subtle conflict between this new voluminous universe of sound and virtually of colour, and the photographers' universe, flat, monochrome, that preceded it. The enchantment, like that exercised by some eyes with a squint, will lose its effect. Colour and depth will advance together along a broad front, and some gullible dramatists succumb to the lure of this convenient commercial theatre. The fact is that stage and screen are incompatible: the craft of the theatre cannot serve the film artist, or vice versa. You could say that these two, the one a craft of breathing and reflection, the other of mechanics and animal life caught unawares, actually do each other a disservice. The film artist becomes awkward when left alone on an empty stage, while the stage artist winces and flags from the effort of constructing a series of little scenes under the magnifying glass, each with the precision of a music-hall act.

Hence, cinematography is racing towards a disastrous state of perfection. In any case, this perfection will not prevent cineastes from creating masterpieces, either by taking advantage of this pseudo-theatre, or by contradicting it. And the surprising result will be that both theatre and cinematography will benefit: cinema, because it will be harder to create a masterpiece when black-and-white no longer provides its astonishing effects of grisaille; and theatre, because playwrights will desert it *en masse* for the theatre of the lens, forcing many third-rate playhouses to close down. The boards will be cleared, leaving the space free to those who love true theatre, reject tired clichés and want to use flesh-and-blood actors as the means to communicate a lethal passion that machines are increasingly powerless to conjure up.

May film remain film and none of its images be capable of translation into any language other than the dead language of the image; may a cinegraphic star still exercise the fascination of a dead star whose pulse of light reaches mankind long after it was emitted; and may the audience for cinematography remain an audience hypnotized by these forces from beyond the grave. But let theatre, which has too long been thrown off balance by the rhythm and tempo of film, recover its prerogative, by which a fat Yseult and an ageing Tristan can move us to tears.

Moreover, theatre and cinema will restore to books that which belongs only to books, and was the cause of our slumber: words, words that are so lovely to read and to hear read, awesome words that in both cinema and theatre had become a substitute for action, the need for which is so imperative that a fine act in a play will leave the audience convinced it has witnessed the prodigy of sets that have the power to suffer, that it has watched the drama with its ears and listened to the dialogue with its eyes. [*Entr'acte*, April 1934. Programme for *La Machine infernale*, at the Comédie des Champs-Elysées Louis Jouvet].

On Tragedy

Tragedy is first and foremost a ceremonial.

An audience, ill-trained by continuous cinematography, chamber radio and shows where the artists devolve authority to mere shadows of themselves, no longer has any notion of ceremonial.

They arrive late at the theatre, disturbing the other spectators and the players. There is no vestige of respect or trace of the atmosphere appropriate to great words and sublime actions, the equivalent of silence.

Moreover, whenever the theatre reverts to being theatrical, that is to say, active, an audience which has been brought up to confuse solemnity with boredom is suspicious of what it sees and describes it as melodrama.

What is new is that the players, who no longer possess the technique (the vital rhythm) or the health-giving practice that belonged to great tragic actors in the past, have confused the proper sphere of tragic and comic acting, which were once quite distinct from one another. The modern actor switches instantly from laughter to tears. Shakespeare has always been the model of a playwright whose performers must be able to supply two masks.

Jean Marais triumphed in *Les Parents terribles* in 1938 because he was not afraid to discard the reserve and fear of ridicule that are paralyzing the stage. He played his part as he imagined it would have been played by one of those *monstres sacrés* whose exaggerated style he knew only from hearsay.

With a profound understanding of realism, he infused the part of Nero, in *Britannicus*, with the same natural style that de Max adopted intermittently, switching from a realistic to a declamatory tone.

I mention him because he was the first leading young actor who has so far had the courage to take the plunge.

Alain Cuny, Serge Reggiani, Gérard Philipe, Jean Marais, Jean-Louis Barrault, François Périer, Henri Vidal, Michel Vitold and the rest are tragi-comedians; and, if one had to categorize Alain Cuny in *Le Bout de la route*, it would be as a great tragic actor on a par with Laurence Olivier or Marlon Brando when they perform the modern tragi-comedies of London and New York.

I may add that drama — not to be confused with tragedy

— contributes to this mixture of genres to which our age owes a new genre. Strindberg, for example, wrote more tragedies than dramas, and more dramas than comedies. As a result, the critics are confused: they do not know which way to turn. They look for a particular tone of voice which is no longer essential (or, rather, they refuse to credit a single actor with possessing a combination of several talents).

The mixture is rarer among young actresses. But it is emerging. In the cinema, Michèle Morgan offers us that wonderful feeling of unease that Madame Garbo supremely commands. The two most characteristic tragi-comic screen actress are Bette Davis and Katharine Hepburn.

Everywhere there is upheaval, change and adaptation to change. And the Greek critics are quite wrong to condemn the new use of old myths, considering, for example, *La Guerre de Troie n'aura pas lieu* as sacriligeous. Such was not the opinion of the Athenian crowd at the Herodes Atticus Theatre.

In *Le Jeune homme et la mort*, I attempted a blend of a different kind: tragedy, drama, comedy and dance. I took as the basis for my venture a work by J. S. Bach, thus demanding a degree of respect that was otherwise lost.

Bit by bit, the masses are joining to celebrate this great union. We must help them and let them know that their taste is sound, not try to convince them that they are wrong.

A Wonderful and Dangerous Weapon in a Poet's Hands

We shall soon be laughing at silent films and at those mouths that open without emitting a sound. It is a pity that monopoly disputes should prevent the discovery of depth (which has been made) from combining with speech. In *Hallelujah* [King Vidor, 1929], a masterpiece of commercial cinema (I saw it one morning at the Madeleine), the brother shouted: 'Rue Vignon' when, with the best will in the world,

I could not imagine him being any further away than the wings of the theatre.

Buñuel's masterpiece *Un Chien andalou* proves that cinema is a wonderful and dangerous weapon in a poet's hands. Buñuel is making a sound film and we must expect one of those starting-points to which young people return when progress and facility, like all forms of comfort, condemn us to a certain degree of insipidness. Like the first Chaplins or the first Westerns, Buñuel's films will gather strength and greatness as and when people believe they are going out of fashion (more dramatic images, the contrast between depth of sound and flatness of vision, harsher voices, etc.)

I have been asked to do animation. I hardly dare use this prodigious medium. A caricaturist might confide the linking drawings to assistants; I could not. I imagine it to be a vast undertaking, a source of ridiculous laughter and maddening misapprehensions. I should depict a tragedy, but it would not be enough for my drawings to move: you would have to find a form of animation that would be as distinctive in style as the drawings.

The case of the gramophone convinces me that poetry is moving into an unknown world. *The subordinate role of machines is going to end. We shall have to collaborate with them.*

I recorded some poems for Columbia. And, instead of making do with a photograph of my voice, I changed it, seeking a timbre that would allow the machine to speak without sounding like an echo.

Hence these records become sound objects. They make the poems that were used unreadable and prove that from now on we must have poetry and music which will be published solely by a speaking machine company.

To return to sound cinema: it is certain that speech, depth and colour will lead to a base form of art; but every form of art is base, starting with the theatre, and exists only through that which is exceptional. [Reprinted in *Arts*, N° 432. October 8, 1953.]

Film as a Medium for Poetry

I cannot understand the naïve question: 'Is cinema an art?'
Cinematography is a very young art which has yet to acquire
its pedigree. It is fifty, the same age as myself. This is old for
a man, but young for a muse, when one considers the age of
painting, architecture, music or theatre. Mediocre films are
not an indictment of cinema, any more than painting,
literature and theatre are compromised by mediocre can-
vasses, books or plays. It would be madness not to think of
this incomparable medium for poetry as an art, even as a
very great one.

One may imagine how overjoyed Shakespeare would have
been, could he have known this machine that gives shape to
dreams; or Mozart if he could have recorded the credits of
The Magic Flute.

Farewell to the last black-and-white films. Colour has
arrived. Some people will use it as a form of tinting, while it
will give others the means to invent a style.

I wish to add something. It is true that the author of a film
is its director. Everything belongs to him. I directed *La Belle
et la Bête*, because I wanted to be the real author of the work.
I was anxious to say this so that no one might think that I
wanted to take the place of my friends. [*Le Livre d'or du cinéma
français*, 1946].

Cinema is, first and foremost, a product of understanding.
You can see, in a film, the mutual trust that prevails from top
to bottom, and one of its greatest assets is provided by a
friendly atmosphere. I am speaking even of the electricians,
sceneshifters and effects men, since there are always among
them one or two extraordinary individuals whose work is
done in obscurity, yet is as essential to continuity of rhythm
as our own (for example, the man who pushes the dolly).

The camera equally registers what is invisible and records
the bad moods of a team as much as the good ones; an actor

who is sincere, but who does not like his part, can mysteriously corrupt the work of a film.

Nowadays, the director is supreme master of a film: he is the one who pulls the smallest details together and gives the impetus that allows a cinematographic work to unfold from one end to the other, without breaking down.

Since you ask, my own case is slightly unusual. I conceive a film as its director and what interests me is the way in which the images slot into one another. I always write out the left-hand and the right-hand column and I attach no greater importance to the text — which I always try to reduce to a minimum — than to the visual style. This is the real style of the film, since it is primarily a matter of writing for the eyes. Marcel Pagnol's film is Marcel Pagnol's writing. A director's film is inevitably my writing translated into another language, and that is the case even when the language is beautiful. There is something halting that comes between my language and the director's.

From now on, I shall try to make my own cinema by myself and even to turn the exaggeration of my mistakes to advantage. Yet it is still true that collaborating with a director exerts a considerable fascination for me. [*Paris-Cinema*, special issue on French cinema, 1945].

Good Luck to *Cinémonde*

From as early as I can remember, I have always written drawings and drawn writing. It was natural for me to express myself through the medium of film, since it represents a model union of those two opposites: it speaks with an image, and the image speaks. This is why, except on one or two occasions, I have never tried to make what is called cinema. I have only tried to make the ends meet, that is to say, to give plastic form to the language of poets, which is a distinct language and not, as people believe, some different manner of using their own.

That is why I have always said that it was not my true craft, that I was not a film-maker and did not consider myself under an obligation to shoot one film after another.

All our colleagues have submitted to the mysterious laws without even realizing they are doing so. Their films are silent and eloquent. They work at one and the same time by virtue of a phenomenon that is undeniable since it is proven (however much what we call reality may *dis*approve) and through words that give the power of speech to those living statues whose birth was foretold by Mussorgsky at the moment of his death: 'One day,' he said, 'art will express itself by means of moving statues.'

When people fail to understand this strange breach in time, the strange perspective phenomenon that was manifest in the persons of Miss Moberly and Miss Jourdain at Versailles, it is easy to answer: a film is all there in a can, it exists, it *pre-exists*. The projector unwinds it for you in the same way as time and space which, oddly confused, only allow us to live little by little, second by second, through events that ought to take place as a whole.

In dreams, the course of events is muddled, the Fates tangle their threads and, freed from our blinkers, we are permitted to live side by side with the dead and in unapprehended circumstances. And, I should say, even to live through *what will be* — which, because of the limitations of our organism, we confuse with prophecy (premonitory dreams). In reality, acts to come do not obey the laws of our realm.

It is consequently essential that such great enigmas, and a machine that permits us to take the liberties of dreams, should have a magazine press that will make them acceptable and conceal the awesome force of these 'forbidden games' beneath some reassuring guise.

Cinémonde is at the top of the list; so I wish good luck to it and to its readers who, as some of their letters demonstrate, are attuned to questions that go beyond Oscars, festivals and mere current events. [*Cinémonde*, N° 1000, October 2, 1953].

Presentation

The youth of cinematography, the speed with which it has succeeded in establishing its place, the fragility of the material it uses to express itself, the dangers inherent in machines, the world of phantoms that it scatters, the audience it reaches and, in short, the numberless problems it raises and sometimes manages to solve, exert a fascination from which it is difficult to escape.

For my part, I find that it provides an ink less dull than the pen's, and the means of shifting a considerable load of manual labour that I carry, which writing prevents me from putting to use. I know very well the objections raised against it. But is it not precisely this industrial mechanism, which discredits it and repels writers, this need to counter the downward force, leading it towards death, that inspires us to make use of this weapon?

The great cinema industry, the film factory, the barrier of censorship and the fortunes that are expended there, are urging it little by little away from taking risks, or what industrialists consider to be such. There is no art without risk. Marco Polo came back from China with a paper lantern and a handful of rice and made a fabulous industry out of them. Why should some young film-maker's efforts not outpace Hollywood, for example, and force it to think again?

Cinematography began at the end. Everything in art that creates a profound impression on us and gives prestige to a civilization, always begins with small editions, little magazines, insult and scandal. A need for instant success drove cinematography, from the moment of its birth, to adopt the style of bestsellers and fashionable novels.

Now is the time when there will be an awakening from this unhappy state of hypnosis. The singular is taking arms against the plural. Some courageous producers are accepting that doors will be closed to them and countries refuse their wares. Societies are coming into being that are no longer subject to conformist fears.

The public laughs at awards and unfair criticism. It looks for life, even when it is to be found at the bottom of the scale.

So who is showing it the way? Who leads it? It has only a kind of collective flair that allows a film conventionally disparaged to clear that obstacle and change conventions. I think that cinematography is too expensive. We must find a system that allows young people to plunge into it head first, feet together. Perhaps the saviour will be 16mm and the economies in its use. Perhaps there will be theatres for showing experimental films. Perhaps one such experiment will be worth duplicating by some large firm and exhibiting everywhere. These are the problems that plague us: at first glance they seem easy enough to resolve, but they seem less simple the closer one looks.

It would be madness to confuse our desires with reality and not to realize that cinematography, considered as art, disturbs an enormously powerful system. So what? Did not three Norwegian parachutists decide the fate of the Reich? I remain convinced that no structure can withstand intelligence and daring.

Consider the theatre. It is in opposition to cinematography. They turn their backs on one another. In the theatre, the actors rule. The author belongs to them. In cinematography, he belongs to us. This is why I experimented with *L'Aigle* and *Les Parents terribles*. In *L'Aigle*, I wanted to make a theatrical film. In *Les Parents*, I wanted to *de-theatricalize* a play and present it to the audience from a new angle, without changing a line.

I think it would be madness to accentuate the divide between two great means of expression. When the author of a play transposes it to the screen, the main thing is that he should transpose it intact and change nobody in it except himself. He has only to think: I walk unseen among the artists playing my parts. I observe them from close to. I put my face into theirs. I creep up behind them. I isolate them. I look more often at the person who is listening than at the one who is speaking. I peep through the keyholes of rooms that should exist around the single room to which we are confined by the frame of the stage.

I recommend those who may take on this work to give a great deal of freedom to their players, and not force them to adopt a kind of conventional film style, where it is apparently accepted that one ought to do nothing and rely solely on the look of the actors. A play that has run for a long time drifts and leaves its moorings. It becomes something else. Film allows you to recapture the helm and eliminate glaring faults that nothing else in the world would successfully correct.

The risk this involves is that an actor in the theatre plays to his audience and takes its temperature as soon as he walks on stage. A film is all of one piece. If the audience is hostile, no subtlety will subdue it. Of course, a film-as-film is still a marvellous thing. The rarest of all. An object of mystery, a chimera. But since cinematography is an art, and a very great one, it is necessary for this art and that of the theatre to join hands.

Let us 'cinematograph' the classics in the way I have said.

These ideas are close to my heart and I am pleased to set them out at the beginning of the first *Almanach du Théâtre et du Cinéma*. As a jotting-pad, a guide and a gesture of complicity, it has come at the right time. I am happy to offer this evidence of dead research through a door ajar on the future. The dream goes on. [*Almanach du Théâtre et du Cinéma*, 1949. Paris, Editions de Flore and 'La Gazette des Lettres', 1948].

Poetry and Films

Some time ago now my first film, *Le Sang d'un poète* had the honour of being psychoanalyzed by Freud. Re-reading his essay, I feel that this is the only possible form of criticism. Indeed, whatever of our shades, our darkness and, in a sense, our poetry we put into a film is not our concern and should only be uncovered by those who judge us. The cabinet-maker's viewpoint is not that of the medium. The one

ensures that the table is firm, that it stands up and its
drawers slide properly; the other makes it turn and speak.
And, just as tables speak, in other words establish a mysteri-
ous link between the darkness and light within us, so a work
of art should also be a work of craftsmanship that yields its
secrets without in the slightest having sought to put them
across. So I would distinguish clearly between a film that
tries to be poetic, and a film where the poetry is incidental.
Moreover, the *poetic* is not *poetry*. It is even probable that they
are opposites. Poetry is a product of the unconscious. The
poetic is conscious. They stand back to back, and a great
number of excursions into the poetic contain not the slightest
poetry. On the other hand there are realistic ventures which
radiate a poetry that bathes them in phosphorescent light.

My only intelligent perception has been to perceive that I
am not intelligent, despite those who tell me I am. Under-
standing comes to me in flashes, glimmers and spurts, while
intelligence combines these flashes and glimmers to produce
a steady light by which forms are given a kind of relief. I do
not have that light and have to make do with those brief
flashes that instantaneously reveal the unexpected arrange-
ment of things. This is why I am suspect and incomprehen-
sible to those who adopt a methodical approach and wish to
take objects in hand, instead of taking them in with a swift
glance.

The cinema-poet's first concern should, therefore, be to
treat a tale or a legend as an everyday device and to believe
in acts of magic as he does in the most routine actions. I
might add that such actions, endorsed by custom, are in fact
as alien as the supernatural occurrences invented by the
mind.

In the long run, mankind has accorded itself the right to
create a world that is superimposed on the visible one and to
make visible a world that is ordinarily invisible. I believe
that this world not only exists in the same sense as the other
and constrains the incredulous to be wary, disquieting them
to the point of revealing dormant senses within them; but
also that it precedes manifestations that are still abnormal,

and are likely to become normal with time.

Since Arthur Rimbaud, poets have ceased to operate merely by charm. They operate by *charms*, using the word in its most dangerous sense. Instead of seducing, the poet terrifies: this explains the battle that is being waged against him. At the moment of waking, he unleashes the forces that govern our dreams and that people quickly try to forget.

Cinematography is a powerful weapon for making men sleep on their feet. The darkness of the theatre and the lunar glow of the screen are quite liable to produce the collective hypnosis exploited by Indian fakirs. [*Filmkunst*, November 22, 1948].

Poetry in Cinematography

I am rather surprised whenever I hear people chatter on about poetry in cinematography, the fantastic in cinematography and, particularly, 'escapism', a fashionable term which implies that the audience is trying to get out of itself, while in fact beauty in all its forms drives us back into ourselves and obliges us to find in our own souls the deep enrichment that frivolous people are determined to seek elsewhere.

This casual use of language, which critics are accustomed to confuse with something profoundly enhancing, is in danger of misdirecting a whole generation of young people who are eager to pick up the expensive pen of cinematography and to express themselves in the ink of light.

The more I try to study the job of film-making, the more I perceive that it is effective on an intimate, confessional and realistic level, and the more I realize that the resources that appear to be its prerogative point us in the wrong direction, so that we lose our way in fantasy and the picturesque, along a dangerous path, misleading to all those who do not comprehend that unreality is itself a form of realism governed by strict laws. There is nothing more precisely detailed and internally consistent than those dream plays whose threads are broken or tangled only because our memories are weak.

A film is not the telling of a dream, but a dream in which we all participate together through a kind of hypnosis, and the slightest breakdown in the mechanics of the dream wakens the dreamer, who loses interest in a sleep that is no longer his own.

By dream, I mean a succession of real events that follow on from one another with the magnificent absurdity of dreams, since the spectators would not have linked them together in the same way or have imagined them for themselves, but experience them in their seats as they might experience, in their beds, strange adventures for which they are not responsible . . .

Researchers who investigate these problems ask unanswerable questions: 'Do you prefer fantastic or realistic films?'; 'Do you prefer realism or non-realism?'; and suchlike nonsense which proves that the people putting the questions have never considered the matter or given it serious thought.

Teamwork is an essential part of the undertaking. A man alone could not manage to operate the factory that puts life in a can, but the ideas of the man who controls a film must be powerful enough for this great machine to obey him.

Each worker tries to contribute the greatest possible amount of work in his own field, while not concerning himself with the whole. And this is true to the point where the specialists who come together in the cinema studio (including the actors) do not look at the film, or listen to it, or take an interest in it, except in as much as it is the product of their own labour.

The spectator who is not involved in the making of a film and attends an evening performance, does the same, either looking for whatever in the plot resembles his own memories, or else refusing to be hypnotized because the assisant's clapperboard and the succcession of similar scenes prevent him from lapsing into imaginative slumber.

A prompter at the Théâtre Hébertot raved over Edwige

Feuillère's feet in *L'Aigle à deux têtes*, because that is all she could see from her box.

One man alone can take in the whole and assess whether the individual efforts have been combined and their responsibilities cover his own, and if what he wanted has emerged from everyone's work.

So you will realize that this man would be in a constant state of anxiety, were he not to lapse into a kind of prostrating slumber and to rely somewhat on the instinct for survival that drives the various parts of his being and forces them to remain alive.

In such a state, even if he has settled the tiniest detail beforehand (because some people follow precisely what they have written, while others improvise on the spot), it would be crazy to think that there is any space left for him to worry about poetry, fantasy and the supernatural. As far as space is concerned, what remains for escapism (as they say) is the professional pride of a cabinet-maker at work on a table, concerned only to ensure that it stands firm, and has properly sliding doors and neat corners.

Afterwards the mediums may come, if they wish: the audience, elbow to elbow in the dark, will put its hands on the table and make it turn and speak by secret means, since the words attributed to tables at séances are lifted out of our own pockets and come from the darkness within us.

The audience's role is huge and has to be relearned. Unfortunately it is losing its sense of ceremonial and solemnity. In the theatre, because of the dozens of magazines that claim to take each of their readers into the wings and the actors' private lives, the crowd is no longer held back behind the burning bush of the footlights, the solemnity of the red curtain, the stage manager's baton that signals the start of the play and calls for an almost religious hush. Everyone comes late, disturbs the rows of already seated people, treads on their feet, talks to the usherette, coughs, spits and, thinking only about transport home, hurries to leave, while the actors who have expended their energies on the public's behalf are taking their bows.

I am happy to concede that French audiences may be unsuited to collective hypnosis, resist it with all their individualistic strength and try to demonstrate their intelligence through criticism. I accept that this perceptive élite should stay on its guard and suspect that you may be taking it for a ride, when you are giving it the blood of your veins and exhausting yourself in an effort to win it round. But, for all that, they should have regard to a minimum standard of behaviour and, simply because they have paid for their seats, this does not relieve them of every obligation or give them a licence to act like pigs.

And if the man who carries out a work of cinematography offers us the essence of his heart and soul, precisely because he cannot control the impulse to do so; if he submits himself to undertaking a humble task and this essence escapes from his innermost being, an essence and charm that owe their effect to the very fact that they are uncalculated; then how do you expect this essence and this charm to work when the audience, his true collaborator, responds with ill-mannered indifference to this proposal of a marriage of love?

If the public goes out of its way to lose its childhood faculties, if it pretends to be an incredulous grown-up unable to slip into that sphere where the unreal becomes matter-of-fact, if it insists on hardening itself against the euphoria it is being offered, if it makes fun of things that are beyond it instead of attempting to raise itself to their level, in short, if it will play the sceptic when confronted with the mysteries of religion and art, I am no longer surprised when people complain that producers are inclined to make only films of the most lethal vulgarity.

This craving to understand (when the world that people inhabit and acts of God are apparently incoherent, contradictory and incomprehensible), this craving to understand, I say, shuts them off from all the great and exquisite imprecisions that art deploys in the solitudes where men no longer try to understand, but to feel.

This is why I am fascinated by cinematography, which goes beyond the little audience for theatre and is that much more likely to reach those few souls in the world who are searching for food and dying of hunger. [*L'Amour de l'Art*, N° 37-38 and 39; *Cinéma*, 1949].

Beauty in Cinematography

Beauty is made up of relationships. It derives its prestige from a specific metaphysical truth, expressed through a host of balances, imbalances, waverings, surges, halts, meanderings and straight lines, the peculiar quality of which is that they should be inimitable and which, as a whole, add up to a marvellous number, apparently born without pain. Its distinguishing mark is that it judges those who judge it, or imagine that they possess the power to do so. Critics have no hold over it. They would have to know the minutest details of how it works, and this they cannot do, because the mechanics of beauty are secret. Hence the soil of an age is strewn with a litter of cogs that criticism dismantles in the same way as Charlie Chaplin dismantles an alarm clock after opening it like a tin can. Criticism dismantles the cogs. Unable to put them back together or understand the relationships that give them life, it discards them and goes on to something else. And beauty ticks on. Critics cannot hear it because the roar of current events clogs the ears of their souls.

Beauty takes the most varied forms, yet wells forth from a single spring. It multiplies and endures through the intermediary of the cubists who serve as its pretext or vehicle, and asks only that they should brace and sharpen themselves to serve it. It avoids those who are in the business of taming or taking it by force. In a sense, it demands the same concentrated and humble labours of us that we demand of the workers in a cinema studio. This is what we have to understand, before we can approach the puzzle of how it can arise in those places from which industry drives it out, indulging in a kind of exorcism in order to avoid it. Because, while its face can sometimes deceive the masses, adopting a disingenuous mask, and slide into the world with the terrible sly grace of a virgin by Raphael, an androgynous figure by Leonardo or an interior by Vermeer, it often comes on stage at the approach of the crowd.

At times, it may also be almost entirely invisible; and, since we are on the subject of cinema, I might quote the example of Orson Welles's film *The Magnificent Ambersons*, in which beauty addresses such a perfect language to the eyes that our critics imagined they were hearing platitudes. This was not their fault. Their souls have trodden too many roads and must have hardened like the soles of feet.

In *La Belle et la Bête*, Christian Bérard, Auric and I, Alekan and the rest of my team, avoided the use of any surface of rubble or barbed-wire entanglement, which is very fashionable and penetrates the hard soles I mentioned. We had to turn our backs on fashion and, since beauty will not come when called, build a trap for it into which its hatred of routine would tell it to fall without exerting itself.

So our role consisted simply in making the implausible plausible, and in fidelity to the style of the great French mythology of the fairy story, that naïve realism which allows one to believe. From start to finish of the film, Christian Bérard showed a genius that I could never adequately commend. Not only did he impress the whole film with that air of truth which turns its back on reality and finds strength only in what is almost a sleepwalker's sense of balance, but the merest detail, the slightest object resting on a table was also deliberately chosen by him on the brink of ugliness, in the manner and sphere of what is facetiously attributed to 'the Gare de Lyon', a manner and sphere that are those of Gustave Doré, a master who hovers dizzyingly on the extreme edge of junk and bric-à-brac without ever falling off.

I am speaking about the Beast's castle which, by a fortunate discovery, we were able to base on the strange park at Raray, near Senlis, where the walls are surmounted by baroque dogs, stags and busts of Italian origin. In the merchant's house, we went back to the region around Tours, and Bérard borrowed the awkward look of my characters from Vermeer and Pieter de Hoogh. A scale model is not important to Christian Bérard: everything comes from his ink-stained hands. He invents, tears up, pulls out, and approves only when he has achieved that natural feel that bad set designers avoid. It was the same with the sets that were prepared for him by Moulaert and built by Carré, which he found distracting and transformed by sheer despair and fury to attain his dream.

Bérard discovers and captures the fire that blazes on evenings when poets and painters disguise themselves, driven to invent by the absence of material.

Surely, without him I could have done nothing, any more than I could without Auric whose sublime music goes far beyond what one can expect from a background score. Admittedly, I obliged Alekan to get rid of the webs, gauze, veils and soft focus that the unitiated consider the distinguishing marks of the supernatural. Certainly, I did ask my actors to perform in the midst of the unexpected as though it was anything but. Certainly, the whole team shared my determination not to fall into the trap of calculated mystification. Certainly, Josette Day played a Princess without losing her peasant simplicity and her gait was inspired only by the metamorphosis of dreams, while Jean Marais denied himself the paraphanalia of horror films and, as the Beast, remained a poor, smitten aristocrat beating his breast and awkwardly seeking the site of his pain. But all this would have been of no avail to me if the fatigues of the work had not moulded it together, and made it unassuming in some sense.

This is what I am saying. The camera will see nothing that it is not shown. It cruelly and faithfully records the least of our faults. On the luminous screen, it will multiply them through a dangerous magnifying glass. When we understood this, we forced ourselves to sleep on our feet and to finish our cabinet-maker's task. The table had to be firm and elegant: it was for others to put their hands on it, make it turn and call down the spirits.

People have criticized me for the candelabra with arms, the living caryatids and the drinking-hand, in short, what is in the tale, which Bérard and I wanted to achieve by only the simplest means, of a kind that are admired in Méliès and, with us, attributed to mischievous cunning. What cunning, for heaven's sake? We made do as best we could and no one (except some specialists and the mass audience) has congratulated us for never once having recourse to mechanics, for never relying on special effects, for having — Alekan, Clément and I — always seen with our own eyes what the camera would film and put in the can. '*Steer clear of magic,*' is what I advise those who believe that the cinema is a machine for manufacturing wondrous things. A wave of the wand is too easy. Marcel Carné, confronted with a métro station, creates as much magic as I do. Orson Welles puts the same amount in the half-light of the extraordinary house in which he places the Ambersons. It is because those awful 'élite' cinemas expect something (do they know what?), that they remain indifferent to the other thing that we give them, which can in no way communicate with their inner chaos. They want a script in a permanent wave. They shall not have it. They want funny pictures. They shall not have them. They want a dream, that is to say something vague. They shall not have it. What they will have, and hard luck to them, is that familiar precision of real dreams which they confuse with the idleness of daydreaming. For the beauty of cinematography is not a separate beauty. It is that of a canvas by Picasso, of Grecian marble, of the Lady with the Unicorn, of a window lit at night, of a bridge over a river, of a mean street. It is impossible for anyone to feel it who does not carry within him the seeds of wonderment to which wonders speak.

But beauty's method is nature's. It is prodigal with its seeds. It does not require thousands of souls to ensure its survival. A few suffice and it takes root in them. And these, it always finds. [December, 1946].

On the Venice Biennale

It is partly the feeling we get that they have been scattered at random across a table, that gives the buildings on the Piazza San Marco the peculiar look of golden treasures stolen from some Doge's pocket and left behind by thieves who did not know what to do with them.

The films in the Biennale were shown in the courtyard of the Doge's Palace. This meant that the audience had to follow the story on another screen hanging across the marble, against the sound of bells from the campanile and the flight of moths. I know this from the murmurs that spread from chair to chair at the time when the pigeons flock, black coffee flows freely and the cinema hoardings topple one after the other at the slightest breath across the Adriatic.

Our work on *Ruy Blas* kept us at the Giudecca Studio until nine o'clock, so we could not see the films.

In any case, a festival adds very little to the perpetual festive atmosphere of a dead city, built on fear and folly like that of a shipwrecked man who tries to heave his worldly possessions above the waves. Nothing in Venice is stranger than the sight of fat businessmen coming out of their hotels, with horn-rimmed glasses and leather briefcases, forced to get in step with mascarades, serenades or other idle diversions.

All the old magnificence is still there, summed up in the Palazzo Dario, which I once said recalled Mme Sarah Bernhardt, sitting on the right and waving to the crowd.

From what I am told, it appears that the pernicious effects of technique are gaining ground, and it is for this reason that machinery continues to dominate the spirit. Only the most recent Italian films — to which the Italians, in any case, attach no importance — have managed to conquer the machine and exploit the discomfort through which the spirit always triumphs.

This is the case with Rossellini's admirable film *Paisà*, where one man expresses himself through a people and a people through one man, with perfect ease. It is also the prerogative of films by Emmer, who tries to base his style on a canvas or a fresco and to use great actors who can give him a Hieronymus Bosch, Giotto or Uccello. His sensibility allows him to put movement into a still work, to endow it with intense life and to make a machine (the camera) serve the soul, by dominating it in some way, so that the techniques of the film-maker and the painter disappear beneath a completely new and completely unexpected spiritual light. This ability to give life to a painting with a travelling shot, the framing of a face, the extreme highlighting of a detail or the camera slowly pulling away, is profoundly moving and obliges us to admit that we in fact understood very little of some masterpiece that we may have thought we knew off by heart.

There are no uniformed police in Venice. Good humour characterizes the bit players who lurk about its sets and stroll through its lovely backstage of winding streets. What use are theatres and cinemas? Everything is theatre for this elegant people to whom each shop is a performance; they eat virtually nothing, and are not outraged, but entertained at seeing the tourists overflowing from the restaurants and cramming themselves on the streets.

This ballet of Carpaccios and Goldonis, this promenade, those night-time processions of gondolas proceeding like a slow stream of lava around a casino of lights, its dome dipping beneath the wooden bridges, in short this continual feast for the eyes, exhorts people not to shut themselves up in a closed hall. Even so, Venice has one model theatre: the Fenice, where my actors in *L'Aigle à deux têtes* will perform for the festival.

One evening, one gala, at a pinch. I repeat, I have not seen the films. And I find it hard to imagine a series of performances on the fringe of this festival which is Venice itself, and from which you are excluded as soon as you step aside. [*Carrefour*, September 8, 1947].

On the *Film Maudit*

It is important to make clear just what we mean by this term *maudit* when we use it of cinematography.

Mallarmé coined the phrase *poètes maudits*, to refer to those whose work escapes from the normal bounds and who cross the line behind which the writings of mediocre poets are confined. These 'cursed poets' defy analysis and critics prefer to condemn them out of hand. Consequently, they do not enjoy the same advantages as what remains *visible*, but become in a sense *invisible* except to those whose eyes can see a long way and who like to examine the soft light emitted by that which is insolent and profound.

The invisibility that Mallarmé calls a curse also occurs when a man tries to go counter to fashion, even the very latest. This is when his invisibility becomes complete because it can no longer benefit from the prestige attached to anything enigmatic. It may be that, after a long period of obscurity in art, the most daring artists are those who dedicate themselves to simplicity. There follows a great moment of loneliness, when art achieves recognition neither from simple minds nor from clever ones.

I consider it a matter of urgency to highlight the problem that is holding cinematography back. Is it not the only art which cannot and must not wait, since the amount that it costs forces it to achieve instant success? Yet for some people — and they are increasingly numerous — cinematography is a marvellous way of giving form to individual dreams, while allowing a great number of people to take part in secret things, to harmonize and drive out solitude. Naturally, when I speak of dreams, I do not mean sleeping dreams, but spectacles that unfold in the darkness of human beings, which cinematography projects with direct light. Thus, the darkness of the cinema comes to resemble that of a human body in which a crowd of individuals are dreaming the same dream together. From the start, or almost, a non-thinking or wrong-headed minority, owning sufficient resources to become a majority, took control. A thinking minority disturbs them. *Their* dream is to destroy this thinking minority and to render it harmless. They have decided that they know the audience and its needs. As they judge the audience according to themselves, they misjudge it. They decree that since cinematography is a popular business and people are stupid, it is essential not to demand the slightest effort from them. This wealthy minority is wrong. The public is much closer to the thinking minority than to the one they represent. This is proved minute by minute, adding further to their discomfiture; but, since they cannot make up their minds to take risks, they refuse to understand the reasons and announce that the cinema industry is in decline and likely to go bankrupt.

The mistake is that cinematography has been considered solely from an industrial point of view. Cinematography is a machine, but what it produces cannot be sold in the same way as a yard of cloth. If producers had had the good sense to lay their best bottles down in the cellar, they would observe that their successes are dead and that some of their disasters (or what they consider as such) might earn them a fortune. A preliminary failure, which is considered final in the cinema, honours a masterpiece. This is not to say, however, that failure is obligatory. We may be deceived by a success due to misunderstanding. Hence, Chaplin's films, which are really Kafkaesque dramas, conquered the audience by farcical comedy and are sometimes accused of not being funny any more, when in fact they are achieving their true stature because drama is prevailing over comedy. Because of this discovery, the non-thinking minority has criticized the masterpiece that epitomizes Chaplin, *Monsieur Verdoux*. The wonderful films of Harry Langdon were of the same kind. Of course, they were not considered amusing. They ruined their producers and their author. They are the ultimate in *film maudit*. *Peter Ibbetson* [H. Hathaway, 1935], *La Force des ténèbres* [Possibly *Night Must Fall*, 1937 — see note on page 75] and *Greed* [E. von Stroheim, 1924] are as many masterpieces that have been buried alive.

It is time to pay tribute to them and to sound the alarm. Cinematography has the right to proclaim its nobility and to break out of a bondage from which so many brave men are trying to free it. An art that is not accessible to the young will never be an art.

People will answer me with figures.

I shall reply with figures. A fear of taking risks is ruining producers. They are shutting the door on the unexpected. The best films arise in difficult circumstances. Russia, Germany and Italy conquered the screen at the worst moments in their history. As soon as countries recover, and get rich, the standard of their films declines. All the more so since the minority I mentioned considers these films bad propaganda and relapses into error.

There is no such thing as film production. It is a joke, as much as the production of literature, pictures or music. There are no good years for films, like good years for wine. A great film is an accident, a banana skin under the feet of dogma; and the films that we try to defend are a few of those that despise rules, heretical films, the *film maudits* housed in the treasury of the Cinémathèque Française. [At the Festival du Film Maudit, Biarritz, 1949].

What We Can Learn from Festivals

You have asked what, in my opinion, can be learned from these festivals which are multiplying at such an impressive rate.

For my own part, I prefer the popular vote. It is more informative, and we rarely find that it does not accord with our own secret preferences. But a festival puts the spotlight on an art which has not gained the recognition in France that it deserves. This is because cinematography is still very young and has only just started to emerge from its roots in the industry and lay claim to the inheritance that rightfully belonged to it from birth.

Festivals help to shake off the laziness that encourages
some people to despise the audience and others to think of
cinemas as dark tunnels, to be gone through absent-
mindedly.

A festival raises problems which the jury tries to resolve
and, while several people are engaged in debate, each of
them reflects others, and the verdict of a few has some
chance of getting close to the verdict of many.

At the Biarritz Festival (*film maudits*) we gave first prize to
the American film *Mourning Becomes Electra*. We were divided
between this and Pagliero's *La Notte porta consiglio*. But
despite the beauty of Pagliero's film, narrated like some Arab
tale, we considered that Pagliero could work with greater
freedom than an American director, who is faced with the
insurmountable obstacles of censorship and excessively large
distribution chains.

So *Mourning Becomes Electra* is typical of the *film maudit*, that
is to say a film with a kind of audacity that nothing can hold
back, showing extraordinary courage in taking risks. What
mass audience has ever heard of the House of Atreus?
Murders and suicides pile up and the actors speak in the
theatrical accents of tragedy.

However, this is film, not theatre, because cinematogra-
phy holds up its awesome magnifying-glass to the minuti of
the plot, and close-ups are substituted for antique theatrical
masks. So, if a lazy audience boycotts the film, a festival will
at least have pointed out its lofty achievement.

The Cannes Festival renders an immense service to the
Seventh Art, because of its importance and the sort of
solemnity that surrounds it. There are dangers which
threaten the event. Sometimes films that have been too
eagerly awaited irritate the critics before they arrive and
become the victims of a momentary injustice. In that case,
justice corrects itself and the festival has still rendered the
service of forcing the work to overcome an obstacle and
prove itself by its own means.

In any case, it is important that the festival is there,
encouraging the runners to take part in the race. The more

often exceptional films gain awards at festivals, the more producers and distributors will lose their fear of a public that they frequently misunderstand, which is only asking them to lead it forward.

PS So many errors have been printed about our festival in Biarritz that I should like to make another small clarification. It was not a matter of showing films that have been a failure with the audience, but films that bad luck has prevented from reaching the audience, and films that distributors are unwilling to release for fear of the audience, which is much more perceptive than they imagine. [*Cinémonde*, N° 787, September 5, 1949].

Cannes

I was delighted with Louis Lumière's title that I was granted as a tribute from the festival organizers: 'Honorary President of the Cannes Festival'. Delighted, because it was a reward for my efforts as active president for two years running and, above all, because — being purely honorific — it did not force me to leave my work and make an appearance (not that I mind living in contact with a milieu in which I have discovered a team spirit and almost a family one), but I have, so to speak, retired from the fray and, moreover, this contact with cinematography always gives me a kind of sadness and regret, like a temptation to revert to habits which are, for the time being, forbidden to me.

But then Favre Le Bret, in a plausible and offhand manner, set me a well-disguised trap. I think he is fond of me and knows that, when necessary, I will give my all. So he telephoned me in my hideaway on the Côte and told me that for the 1957 Festival the jury was to be composed of former presidents, so there was no way I could get out of it.

Very astutely (or so I thought) I replied that I would accept if all the others did the same, certain that at least one of us would have a pressing engagement away from Cannes and so foil Favre's machiavellian scheme.

I was wrong. I suppose that all the former presidents were also moved by the nostalgia for this palace, where flags that do not always get on well together in other circumstances, are entangled by the mistral; and all of them answered the call.

That is why, this year, we are gathering like the ghosts of celebrations past, around a long green table similar to the one at the French Academy.

Since the jury was made up of presidents, I suggested to Favre that none of them should preside. I do not know if he will follow this good advice, but it would relieve us of heavy responsibilities which I know only too well.

I have often said that I belong to the race of the *accused*, rather than of the *judges*, that I hate to judge anything or anyone, to reward some and penalise others. The only prize in that game is a good beating.

But there is the Croisette in the sun, the mauve Esterel, the dark theatre with its machine for calling up spirits, the gatherings in the hotel, the memory of the studios where our sets, put up and taken down in rapid sucession, leave as it were the secret geometry of a mysterious labyrinth . . .

And then, the miracle of comradeship. Even though Max Jacob wrote to me: 'You only know the passion of friendship, you have no sense of comradeship . . . ', he may be wrong, because as soon as I return to this environment which has brought me so many joys and so much heartache, I give in, letting myself go and floating along in an element full of sacred monsters and strange wonders. [*Les Lettres françaises*, N° 669, May 2, 1957].

André Lang has forgotten that the 1957 jury was not made up of Academicians, but of former presidents.

Concerning the scrupulously right-minded telegram that was sent to Maurois, I should like to point out that *Le Salaire de la peur* and *Gate of Hell* made a magnificent journey around the world (in much more than 80 days). If my presidency had really discouraged 'wide distribution', I do not think I should have been granted Louis Lumière's title of Honorary President.

PS One is an appeal for the intellectual freedom of the festival, the other against; we should get it clear. I only spoke for myself. Ask my colleagues. I might add that awards are not designed to help in selling something that will sell on its own, but things that aim slightly higher than purely commercial considerations. Publicity will look after the rest. [*Le Bulletin d'Information du Festival de Cannes*, Nº 5, May 6, 1957].

Gentlemen,

I am playing two conflicting roles at Cannes. As Honorary President I am encouraged to make friendly contact with foreign delegations. As a member of the jury, I am prevented from doing so. But, this morning, our schedule allows me to disregard all that and speak to you as a family. Because the world of the cinema is just that and, although I am not making any more films for the time being, for reasons that are quite unconnected with the cinema and do not at all imply, as some of our colleagues have suggested, an indictment of the excessively commercial pressures of the profession, my loyalty to the festival proves how hard it is for me to do without this family.

Thus I do not stand before you either as president of anything, or as a film-maker, or as a judge, simply as a friend. I might add that I was born in the dock and that a judge's ermine does not suit me at all.

As a friend, then, I dare to say what I feel after a certain number of screenings.

What emerges from the totality of the films that I have seen is the fearful portrait of a younger generation that only seeks external feelings and events; and, if it does not find them, experiences an *ennui* that drives some to the countryside and encourages the rest, in the towns, to look for an escape from their inner void in alcohol.

As you know, gentlemen, the epitome of an external event is, unfortunately, war.

So I am speaking to our — to your — great family in the hope that you will help young people to find a means of escaping this lure of the void and to give us back (I am not talking about morality, or comedy, as you can well imagine) the vital and fierce particularity that is an obligation imposed by the enormous undertaking of a film.

Indeed, this undertaking is now too vast for the job to be performed as a simple, casual routine. The more a film costs, the less in my view it should aim for big returns at the box office, and this is no doubt how it will achieve them.

And, at a time when cinema is also looking towards the outside for the means of revival (which seems to me a mistake, since it is the privilege of art not to depend on progress), the gropings of television may soon give us cause for a radical renewal of ideas.

Excuse me, gentlemen, for speaking frankly. If I do so, it is because the friends I see around me are never guilty of the mistakes that I have pointed out; and the two or three films that, in my opinion, rise above the rest, though they belong to the same dark tribe, are only distantly related to it and in a way that transcends it.

In a world of discord and serious misunderstandings, I would like to express the hope that our international group will give an example of mutual comprehension, and the most open, free and profound friendship. [Speech to the opening of the congress of the Fédération Internationale des Auteurs de Films et de Télévision, *Le Bulletin d'Information du Festival de Cannes*, N° 12, May 13, 1957].

Gentlemen,

The Muse of Cinema is the youngest of all muses and, though I am not yet a centenarian, I can boast of having seen *L'Arroseur arrosé*, *Le Train qui entre en gare* and *Les Bébés sur la plage*, in a little basement across the street from Old England.

I should have been very surprised if anyone had predicted that one day I should put this strange magic lantern to my own use and that, sixty years after my visit to a cellar where a lantern brought things to life, I should have as much trouble making a film as if I had decided to do it then, in my sailor suit, short pants and matelot's hat. Yet it is true. And, without mentioning the obstacles that have arisen between my next film and myself, I mean to talk to you about the origin of these difficulties. Because it seems curious, when films were once made so quickly, that we are still at the stage of driving all of them along the same track and committing the same error as if, for example, no book were ever published without a guarantee that it would sell several thousand copies and win all the literary prizes.

People are sometimes amazed that my old film *Le Sang d'un poète*, and Buñuel's films *Un Chien andalou* and *L'Age d'or* have remained alone of their kind. The explanation is very simple: they came into the world thanks to the generosity of a patron, Vicomte Charles A. de Noailles. Without this aristocratic whim in 1930, they would never have seen the light; and, whatever people may say, a million francs for a young man to do what he liked was given more easily then than 100 million would be given to a young man in 1959. Well, *Le Sang d'un poète* has been showing for 19 years in a little cinema in New York: this is the longest exclusive run ever known, and it might perhaps open the eyes of distributors to the unpredictability of the public mind, the curiosity of huge numbers of young people and the colour of personality compared to the anonymity of commercial pressures.

My hope is that the Muse of Cinema will proclaim her nobility and teach how to make distinctions in the lazy mechanism of distribution. The muses should always be painted in an attitude of expectancy. Their role is to wait: to wait for works to reach minds, in the long term, so that they eventually accede to a royal throne after they have caused outrage — that is to say, when they have changed the rules of the game.

I ask you, gentlemen, why should the young Muse of Cinema be the only one out of step with the rest? We treat her in a very offhand manner, and with some contempt, if we condemn her to prostitution, where she has to put money straight in her pocket, before immediately handing it over to her . . . I was going to say, to her pimp . . . on pain of being dismissed as old and unappealing.

Alas, it is her youth that prevents this muse from taking her place in the illustrious ranks of her sisters. She seems never to have gone to the school where they learned to win approbation in the long run, and instead put herself at once at the disposal of the meanest appetites.

To boast that one knows the audience is to boast of knowing the mysteries of the oceans and the stars.

The audience itself, while it is made up of diverse individuals, becomes together, and as a whole, a very sensitive and instinctive child, quick to sense what inspires laughter or tears. The mystery of poetry may escape it, but at least it is intrigued and, instead of mocking (as what is wrongly described as the élite would do), it meditates for a long time after leaving the theatre. I have known many instances of this. It would be ridiculous to misjudge the masses and to view them in the same way as those who imagine they know the public and that they serve up the only popular soup it deserves. The more we consider it unworthy of consideration, the more likely we are to debase it and put it to sleep; and the poor Muse of Cinema will never inherit the glorious place she deserves, which will have been denied her by a gross psychological error.

This is the direction in which I should like to point your debate. And since this room holds the best representatives of the industry, perhaps you will be able to come to some agreement, so that your noble task will no longer fall into hands that are depriving it of its opportunities and stifling it at birth.

I have often said: 'I know that poetry is indispensible, but I do not know for what.'

And now, gentlemen, if you were to ask me: 'Where is the cinema going?', I should reply (if your question happened to fall on one of my pessimistic days): 'It is going, like the rest of the world, towards the destruction that Nature has designed for it, in order to start again from scratch.'

And if your question happened on one of my optimistic

days: 'There will always be lots of mediocre films and few remarkable ones. And this is all to the good, since biologists tell us that dissymmetry produces life and symmetry is synonymous with death.' And I suppose that like me you laugh when the film industry talks about good years for films, as though it was talking about good years for wine.

Fraternal greetings to all. [Speech made at the inaugural meeting of the Fédération Internationale des Auteurs de Films, *Le Bulletin d'Information du Festival de Cannes*, N° 5, May 4, 1959].

A poet is duty bound to remain an invisible man. Remember Beau Brummell's splendid remark that he could not have been elegant at the races 'because you noticed me.' Transposing this remark to a different plane, I conclude that when a poet receives a honour or title, it is because he has some sin on his conscience and has let himself *be seen.*

However, certain honours and titles are a tribute to this invisibility itself and absolve the recipient of some of his guilt.

The title of Honorary President for life at the Cannes festival and the honour accorded me on May 16, 1960 are of that kind. They owe their worth to the friendship of my colleagues and I see them as further proof that our age despises matters of the heart less than one imagines. I should like to thank the Festival. [*Le Bulletin d'Information du Festival de Cannes*, N° 15, May 18, 1960].

Science and Poetry

This week, I had a good laugh at an article by a young journalist who believes that nuclear science is a fashion, accuses me of 'following it' (*sic*) and compares me to Beau Brummell. Quite apart from the fact that I can hardly imagine Brummell following fashion, this journalist is doubtless unaware that nuclear studies began with Heraclitus.

Only yesterday, the unknown were unknown. Today, unknown artists are well-known, and even famous, while famous artists are sometimes unknown. If this young journalist had been acquainted with my work, he would understand why the Saclay Centre asked me to write the script for its film *A l'aube du monde*. Science and poetry are concerned with number. They are not fashionable attitudes, but organisms which do not permit the slightest inaccuracy or imprecision. The commission originated in a chapter of the *Journal d'un inconnu*, entitled 'On Distances'.

The very closed world of modern science was opened up to me more by this chapter and some problems that have been puzzling me for a long time, than by fortuitous, friendly meetings. This world correctly realized that the statement at the beginning of the film — 'Few scientists have the power of speech' — was not a slur, but meant that our prerogative as poets is to make the abstract concrete, to define the invisible and give it volume and contours, in short, to become the mouthpiece of scientists who, except in a few rare cases (Henri Poincaré or Bergson, for example), are more at home with algebraic formulae than with linguistic ones. Despite appearances, my script shows that my formulae are diametrically opposed to a 'poetic' style. They shun that, aiming simply to facilitate a pleasant tour around some machines designed for very mysterious ends. I worked under the guidance of the Centre. As it happened, I was forbidden to indulge in the slightest flight of fancy (which I hate), but I tried also to avoid the banalities of most guided tours.

When something is further away in space, it grows smaller. When something is further away in time, it seems to get larger. From a plane, a lake becomes a pond, but the ponds of our childhood are remembered as lakes. This is the kind of illusion with which space-time likes to deceive us. Other disconcerting illusions await us in Saclay or Marcoule. But while defence against the malevolence of something infinitely small has mobilized a vast arsenal comparable to antique machines of war, nature, on the other hand, using the methods that Edgar Allen Poe described in

'The Stolen Letter', has disguised one of its most fearful secrets in pastoral innocence.

Like anything profoundly new, the decor of Saclay and Marcoule is not picturesque. Imagine the setting for a play with a fascinating plot, where the audience could only see the wings and the props that were witnesses to the the drama. The Sphinx of atomic power hides its enigmas. It does not show its claws, its rump or its wings. It presents the modest spectacle of a Texan hut from one of those films we saw when we were children.

Prince Louis de Broglie has said that an atomic pile is a bomb operating in slow motion. This brake tames and domesticates monstrous forces. A geiger counter sniffs the rocks like a pig's snout sniffing truffles, and radioactive waste fertilizes the soil dishonoured by bombs.

So it was essential for me to imagine the figures on the blackboard and glimpse inside this strongroom of science, which is more than ever thrice-locked.

Man is a prisoner between three walls and it is on the invisible fourth that he tries to inscribe his loves, calculations and dreams.

No doubt, alas, in my attempts to chalk something on this wall through which prisoners try to escape, I have displayed the awkwardness of a child or a lover. I ask forgiveness and would like to express my gratitude to the directors of the Centre d'Etudes Nucléaires who gave me free rein, criticized none of my shortcomings and even had the good grace to pretend that I had none. [*Les Lettres françaises*, N° 606, February 9, 1956].

Sound Civilization

Everything connected with genius is always considered dangerous — a brilliant invention or a brilliant man. A man of genius is customarily described as dangerous, which means that he has bad imitators. But that is not the fault of

the man of genius. Genius cannot be banned on the grounds
that it opens the way to errors. At present, everything that is
invented belongs to a realm of genius that is necessarily
dangerous, but one cannot condemn it. It would be ridicu-
lous to do so. Radio is pernicious if it flows into every home
like a stream of lukewarm water. It is very important if it
brings culture to people who had no conception of culture.
All this seems patently obvious to me, but some people say
that radio is essential, and others that it is harmful. Radio is
neither essential nor harmful. It is an invention of genius,
and consequently a dangerous one. Everything useful may
be considered useless. Poetry, for example, is naturally
useless; but it is not beautiful for that reason. It is beautiful
because it is a distinct language, not a dead language, but a
living language that seems dead. It is a language that takes
time to unravel. People are accustomed to assess everything
against a single measure of speed. There are many different
kinds of speed. People always judge things as a whole and
say 'radio is good', or 'radio is bad', when it would take
hours to explore the matter.

It is certainly true that individuals have been influenced
by the world of sound, but sometimes for ill, because the
radio is so widespread and extensive that it tends to obey: to
obey its listeners, when it would be better if the listeners were
to obey it. In other words, if one could manage to reach a
high level of creation through sound apparatus, this would
be an excellent achievement. But unfortunately, since one is
constrained to go along with the present moment in fields
such as this, there is a tendency, as I have said before, to
respond to demand.

It would be difficult to create a living radio as long as it
requires written scripts. Reading gives the radio a sort of
tedious banality, even with an expert reader. It is above all a
medium of improvisation. On the other hand, I know that it
is impossible to base a programme on chance. These are the
reasons why I have never seriously thought about radio.

Radio is terrifyingly intimate. The whole problem is that it
has to enter a room and impose itself in such a way that those

who listen to it set aside whatever was on their minds, and let themselves be captivated by whatever is on ours. An off button is so easy to turn. On the other hand, if the radio is just a background accompaniment to people's own private concerns, it loses all interest and becomes just another tap in the house.

I am sorry that sound reproduction and cinematography are not more widely used for educational purposes in schools. Voices are obviously more striking than a text read out aloud, and it is more pleasant and more effective to learn from pictures, for example in a subject like history. Children should be shown slow-motion films of plants and flowers, and Painlevé's films on the birth of a butterfly and a sea horse. I cannot understand why all schools are not equipped with 16mm projectors, as well as long-playing records or tapes — and not for simple entertainment, outside the syllabus.

The universe of sound has been enriched by that of ultra-sound, which is still unknown and may remain so, since we are limited to the registers that our senses can perceive and our brain record; but this does not prevent us from realizing increasingly that our little world is situated in the midst of another, vast world; and that it would be naïve to think that the progress we make takes place within clear, easily defined limits, however astonishing it may be.

Doctors have just relieved me of very acute pain by means of the ultra-sonic device invented in Germany and perfected at a factory in Vence. Science tells us that there will soon be ultra-sonic bombs, next to which the H-Bomb will seem trivial. We must hope that all these mysterious weapons will become so deadly that peace (a synonym for war) will lose its symbolic meaning and nations will arm themselves against war.

It is no less true that this widening of the audible universe, which will doubtless be followed by a widening of the visible universe (though I cannot tell how), will only bring us a misappropriated use of wealth that is forbidden on our scale of values. We shall know that fish shout, that the sea is full of noises and that the void is peopled with realistic ghosts in whose eyes we are the same. We shall perhaps be able to extract the past that has been recorded by matter and learn that the past and future are only an illusion of perspective, but we shall still have to live every minute and return after our deaths to that inconceivable world which we inhabited before we were born. I mean that it will be somewhat disconcerting for man to know that he is surrounded and hemmed in by invisible and inaudible forces, the existence of which will be proved by the effects that he produces either to heal or to destroy. Curiosity lures me more, I admit, towards these problems than towards those of perfecting the visible and audible universe. The reason for this is no doubt that I have taken a very long time to adapt old methods to my use and I am always a little awkward when I have to turn to new ones which seem to outstrip the rest.

The greatest mistake is believing that the one does outstrip the other. The idea is laughable. In this respect, our age will be as comic as 1900, which now makes us laugh, while the important, slow things in every age do not progress. Picasso has not overtaken El Greco, Rembrandt or Van Gogh, he has put more riches into the treasure-house. Belief in speed is a superstition of our age. Just as people have the urge to overtake one another on the roads, so they say that an artist has been 'left behind'. Besides, everyone ends up at the traffic lights or in hospital.

In my own field, we walk, and always shall. When speed goes by, intoxicated with itself, if it spatters us with mud and light, the main thing is not to doubt our legs and not to thumb it down, or else we may be picked up and become *engagés*, to use the fashionable term, 'committed' to ride in a vehicle where we do not belong.

One day, men will be horrified to realize that their cells are as distant from one another as the stars, that they are infinite, a sort of cloud or, more precisely, a fishing net criss-crossed by those waves of sounds and images that we can neither hear nor see. [*La Revue du son*, N° 7, October 1953; *Arts et Techniques sonores*, N° 29, October 1953].

In Praise of 16mm

France is a country of dialogue. Its refusal to obey the rules, its traditional anarchism and almost pathological individualism incline it to the opposite of monologue. People here are always debating, arguing and quarrelling. Outsiders are astonished by this spectacle and find France an enigma. If France stopped arguing, or even continually contradicting itself and existing in a state of effervescence, if it were to accept the sort of monologue that killed Hitler's Germany and will kill any nation that submits to it, it would die and sink beneath a weight of dullness that its internal structure does not at present allow to crush it.

Its flashes of light are sparks struck out of apparent disorder. I might add that it is fortunate that those who govern us have not noticed this and contribute to the great richness of the disorder without understanding it. No doubt, if they did understand, they would try to do deliberately what they achieve unconsciously and, at that moment, the mechanism would become highly pretentious and cease to operate effectively.

Far be it from me to suggest anything so methodical. I observe how efficiently this has worked with us for centuries. Perhaps it would not work abroad — but our French cock can only crow on a dungheap. If they were to clean up the farmyard and remove its pedestal of gold and dung, it would die.

In my view, a capacity for dialogue is of vital importance to a nation. The main danger confronting cinematography, not only in France but in all the countries of the world, is the amount that it costs and the fear of taking risks imposed on us by the money that producers invest.

This deprives cinematography of those contrasts, experiments, flights of daring and marvellous failures that allow art to overcome inertia and to break with habit, which is always fatal to it.

At present in France, where there is a minimal distribution circuit, a producer who wants to make 14 million francs (on which he has to pay a massive burden of tax), must invest 100 million to start with; and of those the film costs him 60 million.

If he does not give up the job, it will be because he is caught up in the business and hangs on against his better judgement. Little by little, he becomes a patron and a very bad-tempered one, which is understandable, because that was never the role he chose to begin with.

I repeat that, in my view, the danger threatening American cinematography is the same as the one that threatens our own. In America, the danger must be worse because a film's huge sales and the publicity that it represents make the film companies inclined to stray as little as possible from what they believe to be the right path. This cuts off the sap, that is to say, young people: who would dare to risk such sums on ambition that has not proved itself? Yet, as we all know, art has survived only because of little volumes with small sales in their time, little newspapers distributed by hand and magazines with minimal print runs. This is where the world later finds the names that it respects and loves. This is where the seeds are nurtured that scatter afar and germinate. This is the chamber music composed in the dark from which the world derives its great rhapsodies.

I ask you, what constitutes the glory of France? Certainly not its politicians, but Villon, Rimbaud, Lautréamont, Verlaine, Nerval and Baudelaire. France despised them, hunted them down, let them starve, commit suicide or die in the public wards.

We have to protect this mysterious heritage. We should fail to recognize the importance of cinematography and not understand that it is an art *on the way to becoming the completest art*, if we were to treat it like a factory for luxury goods and not try to put its life-giving weapon into everyone's hands.

An art in which young people cannot freely take part is condemned from the outset. It is vital that the camera should become a pen and that everyone should be able to express himself through this visual medium. It is vital for everyone to learn editing, shooting, montage and sound, not to become specialized in one branch of this very difficult trade, in short, not to be a single cog in one of the machines in the factory, but a free body which can leap into the water and find out how to swim by itself.

I cannot imagine any young person nowadays being presented with an opportunity such I was given, eighteen years ago, when I was allowed to make *Le Sang d'un poète*, with no technical help and without having ever set foot on a set.

This was the whim indulged by a man who was eager to escape from the common run, the Vicomte de Noailles. But, despite what people say, the rate of exchange is not relative and 12 million francs[1] would be put up less readily now than a million then.

In any case, who in 1948 would pay out an amount equivalent to that million francs, to let a young film-maker do what he wished, without any material, artistic or moral constraint?

So I was lucky and what I demand is the same good fortune for those of the same age and daring as my own at the time.

In my view, 16mm film is the only means of solving the problem and I believe that America should take the initiative. It has an asset — volume of business — that will permit it to accept small marginal sales. Moreover, these small sales may become very large and surprise those who take on the risk.

American 16mm cameras are astonishing; they are likely quite soon to have sound. In the event, it would be better for this development to be delayed as long as possible, because sound tends to adhere lazily to the image, and the use of sound as an effect, invented sounds dubbed on to the image, would excite the imagination of young innovators.

When I use it, 16mm film, which I have just shot in my

---

1   'Old' francs. From 1960, 1 (New) Franc = 100 (old) Francs.(Tr)

garden, takes things to extremes. Liberated from any mate-
rial considerations, since I was using Kodak reversible film
and since what normally amounts to five million francs cost
me five thousand, I made a film which was not in the
slightest a film. I invented as I went along, improvising
minute by minute and using the people who happened to be
spending Sunday with me in the country as actors. The
result was a series of fairly ridiculous, and unusable scenes;
yet this complete freedom to say whatever came into my
head gave them a power that would be impossible to obtain
if it were a question of bankrupting a film company.

Picasso is probably the only man in the world who can
make a marvellous object out of nothing: a piece of wire, the
carcass of a dead animal or a bicycle saddle. Hardly has he
touched these scraps than they take on new meaning and
sparkle in that other world that belongs to him alone: he
appoints them princes in his kingdom. With 16mm film we
are allowed to risk such miracles. A close-up, an unexpected
angle, a wrong movement, fast or slow motion, or running
the film backwards are enough to make objects and shapes
start to follow us and obey, as the creatures obeyed Orpheus.

Because we showed our first cut over the overture to
Coriolanus, I called the film *Coriolan*, and I intend eventually
to give it a soundtrack and a commentary as far removed
from what is depicts as its title. It is possible that that joke
will never see the light of day. It may slip through my fingers
and escape, for lots of other people subsequently to find a
host of meanings in it that are not there, or perhaps are,
unknown to me.

Any number of interpretations have been discovered in *Le
Sang d'un poète*. Is this my fault? I am a cabinet-maker. I make
a table. I am not a medium. If other people make the table
turn and call up messages out of it, messages that must come
from within themselves, they are playing their part as an
audience and I have no objection to that. So I hope, with all
my heart, that Hollywood will associate a minor branch to
its great enterprise of film-making, one that will not be
protected against routine by any insurance, but invite acci-

dents to happen. Because it is an 'accident on the line', or some terrible shock, that gives birth to those works that will one day resound to the honour of mankind.

January 1948: PS — What I am talking about, naturally, is commercial exploitation of 16mm films in specialized distribution circuits and theatres. (This postscript was added by Jean Cocteau after the *New York Times* had requested clarification).

Great Sixteen

The 16mm format will allow young people to express themselves in a manner that is impossible through the 'offical' media. Too expensive! Too heavy! But there are profits to be made on a film costing sixty million francs; there is no surplus value on one of sixty thousand. This is the secret behind the struggle of big business against the hand-gun.

An actress making a 16mm film tells me that she is put off by not having a heavy camera in front of her, by the substitution of a keyhole for a bull's eye. A bad habit has already been learned.

Film-makers must resist this tendency of cameramen, reverse it and force them to follow us *down the wrong path*.

Hollywood shouts: 'Help!' The answer is simple: America must offer young film-makers distribution outside the main circuits, relieve them of the crushing responsiblities of the major studios and support the 16mm format. *I am not thinking of an experimental undertaking, but an industrial one.* Those who commission a 16mm film are quite at liberty to reformat it on 35mm if the audience responds, as it probably will, since it is never given the chance to escape from a track which is supposedly the only one on which it can travel.

A film that is designed to please the audience almost always fails. On the other hand, when a producer allows himself the luxury of a 'marginal film', it will often go a long way on public acclaim. Then, this despised film rises to the top and takes others with it.

You may argue that there is the problem of sound. Is it really a problem? At the moment, sound clings too tightly to film, dragging it back. If the poet film-maker was forced to resort to post-synchronisation, he would have to use sound humorously and inventively, which is what happened at the start.

At my home in the country, I made a 16mm film, *Coriolan*. I made it on 16mm to avoid the temptation of duplication (that is to say, of commercial use) and so that I would not be constrained in any way in my visual writing. The result is a farce, but one that is far more concentrated and intense than any of my 35mm films. Because, even though I 'know the score', I can still become the prisoner of a big firm and a large crew.

The taximetre clicks on, and the millions pile up; yet I owe it to myself to be economical, in the best and worst senses of the word.

The cutting of a film has to be worked out down to the smallest detail. At the last minute, I suggest changing everything, according to the miracles that life, the set and the actors have wrought. It would be crazy to subject so many things that are dependent on chance to a preliminary design which may win favour in the office, but not on the set.

The real is not the truth, and it is the truth that counts.

The boom operator should be a musician, not a fisherman.

Technicians have puzzled in an attempt to discover how I filmed Marais' fall at the end of *L'Aigle à deux têtes*. The trick was very simple: there is none. He falls backwards. Cinematography allows you to capture a daring stunt that the actor would not repeat a second time.

There have never been so many precise analyses as those about *Le Sang d'un poète*, in which I did 'whatever I liked'. This 'whatever' has a *meaning* for each individual. In the film, I sleep on my feet. It is the story of a sleepwalker, but not of a dreamer. In that state of dozing in front of a fire, when the mind wanders, I express myself through signs. To describe it as 'a surrealist film' is laughable, and only proves the ignorance of historians of the mind.

Even before *Le Sang d'un poète*, twenty years ago, I made the first film in the spirit of 16mm. Where has it gone? It has vanished without trace. Braunberger is looking for the reels, because he saw me working on the film at the Studio des Cignognes. A fat lady was in charge. One day, when the electricity was not working, she said: 'Wait a bit, it will come through in the end.' I had dipped the sheets that my actors were wearing into tubs of water. One of them caught pneumonia. I left the Studio des Cigognes and the lady who thought that electricity travels slowly down a pipe.

You young people, who go to the shadow theatre and emerge with your heads buzzing, you should express yourselves with this light pen and not fear the barbed-wire fence that has been set up around a pseudo-mystery. The mystery is in yourselves and writing with pictures will let you expel it if it is stifling you. Find a friend with a 16mm camera. If necessary, hire one. Set out with its obtrusive magnifying-glass and crowbar. Break into souls. Open up faces. Don't let any technical considerations intimidate you. There are none. You have to invent them. I shall be more moved by your spelling mistakes than by a grammatical exercise. The errors in *Le Sang d'un poète* are often cited as innovations. I had no idea. I did not even know that you could use rails. That is why Chaplin was astonished by the poet slipping into the darkness of the mirror. We moved him along on a platform with a cord, and I resorted to the same primitive device when Beauty glides along the corridor in the Beast's castle.

Wander around anywhere and don't play at being film-makers; leave the uniform behind. Remain free in a world where freedom is hounded down, alone in a world where individuals abandon their individuality to the group, alert in an inattentive world, fearless in a world driven by fear.

Shoot, shoot. Project. Project yourselves out of the dark. Above all, remember that cinematography is realistic, and so are dreams. Everything depends on the order in which reality is cut and reassembled to become your own. [*St. Cinéma des Prés*, N° 1, 1949].

Don't neglect the language. Cinematography hates confusion. A close-up is the mask of classical tragedy. The script also goes under the microscope.

Always choose the warmest scene, even if the framing is less perfect or if it shows the shadow of the boom.

Everything jumps out through the camera, the atmosphere of the set as much as the rest. You can sense a unit's bad temper on the screen. Keep your team in good spirits.

Once I have chosen an angle with the cameraman, I almost always follow the scene from a quite different one, so that I am surprised by the rushes.

The cameraman is our real aide.

The public imagines that cinematography is a toy, an apprenticeship in luxury and idleness. They would be very surprised to learn that these films, which they gulp down like a glass of beer at a bar, are the result of labour that devours us, not leaving us a minute's freedom. Seen close up, the life of the stars is hell. The director's less so because, while in the theatre we belong to the actors, in the cinema they belong to us and become the ink in our pens.

However, it is a fact that people who visit a film set cannot stay there long and are in a hurry to get away. Every second is precious for us, yet the visitor gains nothing from this bustling ants' nest except an impression of waiting and emptiness, dust, tropical heat or icy cold. Hustled from one side to the other, he looks with dread at this place which is not a place, this time which is no time, these ghostly actors and this theatre filled with a jumble of technicians, furniture, lights, make-up artists, half-constructed walls and ceilings that disappear on command. He tries to find out by what miracle these ruins, these constant removals, this exhaustion and dusty grime will release the images of a film, with their glittering, starry solitude.

Nothing is so ludicrous as people who talk about *cinematographic production* and say, for example, that output is falling.

There has never been any such thing as cinematographic production, any more than artistic or literary production. In reality, there are such things as mediocre output and very good routine production — and a few accidents that go with it, which are very rare, but commoner in cinematography than in painting or writing.

For every film by Wyler or Orson Welles, how many brilliantly mediocre films there are, which allow the films of these heroes of the screen to emerge, and without which they would be impossible.

Peter Ibbetson and *La Force des ténèbres* are two examples of ordinary films that rise above the norm. Two masterpieces, but from the American point of view, two failures.

Picasso used to tell me: 'After a certain point, one cannot do *no matter what*: everything one does becomes meaningful.' This is the advantage of a place like Saint-Germain-des-Prés where the state of mind and general atmosphere limit the work of a single man and give a definite advantage to those who are starting out. First find, then seek: that is the way. A milieu where everyone experiments will inspire the mind to discover things at once, without any individual research. Then, as Picasso said, 'all work becomes meaningful, whatever you do.' [*St. Cinéma des Prés*, N° 2, 1950].

II Notes and Tributes

. . . Honestly, the more I think about it, the more afraid I am of
forgetting something, or of some imprecision!

I even wonder if I should get to the end of the list
without mentioning films that would astonish the experts
(for example, I consider *Love Parade* [Ernst Lubitsch, 1929]
a masterpiece).

Apart from that, Chaplin and Buñuel (*L'Age d'or*) seem
to me the only films worthy of the poor muse whom we
never allow to wait: this is the role of the muses, to stand
and wait.

Just think, I almost forgot Stroheim's *Greed* and the
extraordinary film adapted by R. Montgomery from
L'homme qui se jouait la comédie. In France, I believe, it was
called *La Force des ténèbres*[1]. My reply would not be in any
way adequate to the needs of your questionnaire.

We should have to sit down together and make a list on
the back of an envelope . . . [Brussels Festival, 1958].

---

1   Possibly *Night Must Fall* (1937), in which Robert Montgomery played the lead.
None of Montgomery's films as director seems to fit. (Tr.)

Brigitte Bardot

I have always preferred mythology to history. History is composed of truths which become lies, mythology of lies which become truths. One characteristic of our age is that it creates instant myths in every field. The press is responsible for inventing people who already exist and endowing them with an imaginary life, superimposed on their own.

Brigitte Bardot is a perfect example of this odd concoction. It is likely that fate set her down at the precise point where dream and reality merge. Her beauty and talent are undeniable, but she possesses some other, unknown quality which attracts idolators in an age deprived of gods. [*Stop*, October 1962].

What is my business? Would you believe it if I said: all forces, great and small, which drive the world? There are no minor themes for a Baudelairian poet, and anything can serve as an excuse for meditation, which has succumbed to the pace of modern life.

It seems to me too simple, merely to shrug one's shoulders when one sees the masses following the scent of a young actress, their tongues lolling, like a pack of hounds. Every success deserves study, because there must be some reason for it and these reasons tell us about the soul of an age. The soul of our own is remarkably close to the skin. Look at that ravishing little blonde witch astride her broomstick. Watch her fly towards the sabbath. See that sulky young sphinx with the perfect body. Fashion houses can spend a fortune, but that witch or that sphinx has only to buy a pair of pants or a man's sweater at Mme Vachon's in Saint-Tropez, and all the young girls on the Côte will follow that style, and that style will become the fashion. So, at one time, Mlle Chanel prescribed the shape best suited to her own charm, which was that of a peasant girl from the Auvergne, and made it luxurious by decorating the wool with emeralds and pearls.

I am not well acquainted with Mlle Bardot. But, apart from the fact that she exploits the technical skills of a dancer, I believe her to be quite self-effacing, to judge by the way that she strolls around on holiday and does her shopping without an escort of photographers. In any case, is a star responsible for her escort? Is it her fault if she is pushed on to the stage, or blinded with lights? It is easy enough to blame her for it afterwards.

No. Fate made Brigitte Bardot the archetype of a younger generation which takes its style from 'dangerous liaisons' and would laugh at the conscience of the Princesse de Clèves, whether we like it or not. So be it.

André Bazin

Health and drudgery make it very hard for me to write, but I have no fear of spilling ink when it flows from the heart.

I loved André Bazin for the frailty that has taken him from us. His erudition, which I often drew on, was never pedantic.

He knew how to love and would not immediately shy away from anything that went beyond his own boundaries. I have seen him at work in the midst of that free-for-all of the Cannes Festival. He was a shadow. But that shadow had moral strength and I could rely on it without seeing the shadow become a diplomatic silence. He approved of my refusal to pass judgement. In short, he belonged among the accused, because he knew that it is often innocence that is accused and that art, particularly cinematography, suffers most of all from a lack of innocence.

André Bazin was noble and pure, incapable of a base deed. As with Robert Bresson, I should hate to start work on a film without asking his advice.

Now I am alone and sad. [*Cahiers du Cinéma*, N° 91, January 1959].

Jacques Becker

Jacques Becker was a friend — and I do not say that lightly, because I do not jest about friendship. He was my friend because I liked his films, admiration being for me only a kind of friendship, a mixture of head and heart that I am unable to define.

Jacques Becker's speech was hesitant and confused, so that I have known him to become entangled in it to the point almost of silence, a vague murmur in which his fear of expressing himself badly was endearing, like a child when it wants to share something precious.

His childlike soul endowed him with a charm that was powerful, but inexplicable. I feel pain at his loss, but can hardly believe in it, since he endures, faithfully reflected in his films. [*Cahiers du Cinéma*, N° 106, April 1960].

Robert Bresson

In our terrible craft, Bresson is 'in a class of his own'. He expresses himself through cinematography as a poet does through his pen. There is a massive barrier between his nobility, his silence, his gravity and his dreams, and a world where they are interpreted as uncertainty and obsession. [Preface to *Robert Bresson*, by René Briot, Paris, Editions du Cerf, 1957].

Charlie Chaplin

Hôtel Welcome, Villefranche-sur-Mer

Cher Monsieur,

What with idleness, fishing and work, I have very little time to answer you, but I should not like you to think that my silence is inspired by any resentment of your questions.

In brief, I think that the *accidental* beauties of cinema have contributed a great deal to our sustenance (volume, speed, etc.). I would add that I am moved by the films of Harold Lloyd and Zigoto: their poetry goes beyond laughter. Chaplin has too often been told that he is a poet, so he has tried to become one. This is a pity.

Faithfully,

Jean Cocteau.

Excuse this hasty PS, but I have just been to Nice and seen Chaplin's latest film, *The Gold Rush*, and I am ashamed of my reservations. It is an unqualified masterpiece.

Jean Cocteau. [Reply to an enquiry on 'literature, contemporary thought and the cinema' in *Les Cahiers du mois*, N° 16-17, 1925, a special issue entirely devoted to cinema].

When I watch Chaplin's old films, I no longer laugh in the same way. I think of Kafka.

It is normal that this great arc, with *The Gold Rush* at its apex, should finally reach the admirable *Monsieur Verdoux*.

I once asked him: 'Why are you sad?'

He replied: 'Because I have become rich by playing a poor man.'

But, while he has made the invisible visible to all, he has kept a dark corner in himself that nothing can compromise.

This shadow will fall across his last works. It will repel those who criticize him for taking refuge in it. [*Les Lettres françaises*, April 3, 1952].

Mon ami Charles,

Isn't it odd that people should maliciously require a miracle to explain itself; that they should corner it and reduce it, not to silence, but to words? Isn't it odd that human malice should drive a fabulously elegant creature into a trap (or, if you prefer, into a large coffer)?

Once, on the China seas, you lamented to me: 'How many kicks have I had to take before I could say what I wanted to say?' You had just confided this to me, when a complete stranger came over to our table and clapped you across the shoulder. You went as pale as the tablecloth and said: 'That's what I get.' I recognized the incident in *Limelight*.

Outside the cinemas where your film is showing, there are posters: 'Charles Chaplin's first great dramatic role.' What kind of roles have you ever played, except dramatic ones? You are the surveyor of Kafka's *Castle*.

Je t'embrasse. [*Cinéisme*, N° 1, January 31, 1953].

James Dean

Disobedience may be described as the greatest luxury of youth, and there is nothing worse than those times when young people are too free, and consequently denied the opportunity to disobey. In my view, James Dean is a sort of archangel of rebellion against custom: was not death his finest act of disobedience, in its terrible rejection of his promised fame? It is as if he left the world like a schoolboy escaping from the classroom through the window and poking his tongue out at his teachers.

Moreover, all young people who are denied disobedience because they lack orders and hierarchies, are also deprived of mysticism and look around them for an ideal which will be the model of their dreams in flesh and blood.

For all these reasons, James Dean gives sustenance to those souls in limbo between a dead civilisation they have never known and a civilisation in the making that they cannot yet enjoy.

A fantasy, a dream, a young man whose passage was too swift to clog any of the mechanisms of his flight: that is James Dean; and that is why an adolescent throng has raised a statue to him in snow, more enduring than many in marble.

Cecil B. De Mille

Ladies and gentlemen,

We must have done once and for all with a misconception that is impeding the progress of the cinematographic art. This is the mistake of believing that novelty resides in subjects, when in fact it can only come from the manner in which they are treated. It is like saying that I don't like soldiers when I am confronted with Van Gogh's zouave, or that I am allergic to roses when I see a bunch of roses by Renoir.

It matters no more whether the subject of a film is original than the model in the work of a painter, and it is a shame that this misunderstanding persists at a time when both abstract and cubist painters have reduced the role of the ostensible subject to an absolute minimum.

Cecil B. De Mille was a crank, one of those wonderful madmen who think they have a mission and want to convey it to the world at any cost. But it was not this naïve ambition, which extended to ordering himself a pitchfork worthy of King Marsoule, that makes Cecil B. De Mille a prince of the screen. It is his style, his bold, childlike handwriting, his downstrokes and capital letters.

When I was young, cinema was despised and considered a trivial pastime. Suddenly, like the Ballet Russe, two works changed all this and Parisian intellectuals gathered every day, several times in succession, in two small cinemas on the boulevards where one was showing the first great cowboy story with the thoroughbred features of William Hart, and the other was showing *The Cheat*. It is possible nowadays that we would smile at the garden party and the great scene with the red-hot iron . . . But it was *The Cheat* that made 'Cinema' the name of a muse: thanks to these two films, cinema became cinematography and acquired its patents of nobility overnight.

Another thing. Genius is the phenomenon of constantly sanctifying faults which cease to be faults because of the force with which an artist asserts them and renders them exemplary. I would give any perfection in exchange for certain notable faults that imply Van Gogh, Cézanne or Picasso breaking the rules, when perfection implies Meissonnier, Bail or any number of other artists who were supposed to be protecting France from being besmirched by those who were subsequently to bring her honour.

For me, Cecil B. De Mille's very considerable bad taste stands well above what is called the good taste of French moderation; and here, I am proud to quote what Péguy said of me: 'He knows how far one can afford to go too far.' Is there a more precise definition of the boundary within which the craftsman in us controls the schizophrenic?

There is certainly folly in Cecil B. De Mille, and even what is called *la folie des grandeurs*; but, as Tristan says of his love for Yseult, it is a fine folly.

Little by little, it will be understood that art is rebellion against dead rules, whatever the manner in which it rebels. And if Cecil B. De Mille's refusal to submit to intellectualism and the wisdom of common sense has been confused with submission to the demands of the public, we must salute today the sublime obstinacy that he brought to the communication of his dreams.

Marlene Dietrich

Of course, you cannot introduce Marlene, but we can hail her and thank her for being what she is. It is rare for anyone to step straight into myth, as it requires, fully armed from head to foot. Marlene, like a child playing at knights on horseback, rode into her own myth astride a chair.

Those who had the good fortune to see her, when they were quite unprepared for it, astride that chair singing *Ich bin von Kopf bis Fuss auf Liebe eingestellt*, have a memory of perfection.

And why was this perfection not only a staggering deluge

of sex appeal? It is because if Marlene were to do a
strip-tease and, as usual, go right to the limit, nothing would
remain of her except the essential, which is a heart of gold.

For this bird of paradise, this ship in full sail, this marvel
of grace whose feathers, plumes and furs seem to belong to
her very flesh, is a rare weapon, a militant act of kindness
that does not hesitate to cross the ocean to do a favour.

It would be ridiculous to say more, or to take advantage of
the honour that she has done me in allowing me to talk to
you about her. Better to welcome the woman herself, whose
name starts with a caress and ends with the lash of a whip:
Marlene . . . Dietrich. [address read by Jean Marais at the
Bal de la Mer, in Monte Carlo, August 17, 1954].

Marlene Dietrich: your name starts with a caress and ends
with the lash of a whip. You wear feathers and furs which
seem to belong to your body like the fur of a wild animal or
the feathers of a bird.

Your voice and your look are those of the Lorelei; but the
Lorelei was dangerous. You are not, for the secret of your
beauty consists in taking care of your heartline. It is this
heartline that sets you above elegance, above fashion and
above style: even above your reputation, your courage, your
manner, your films and your songs.

Your beauty speaks for itself, so I do not need to speak
about it; I shall salute your goodness of heart. It shines out,
illuminating from within the long tide of glory that you are, a
transparent flood that comes from afar and generously
deigns to extend as far as us.

From the sequins of *The Blue Angel* to the evening dress of
Morocco; from the meagre black dress of *X27* to the plumes of
Shanghai Express; from the diamonds of *Desire* to an American
army uniform; from port to port, from reef to reef, from flood
to flood and from one sea wall to the next, it brings us, in full
sail, a frigate, a figurehead, an oriental fish, a lyre-bird, an
incredible, a marvellous . . . Marlene Dietrich.

S. M. Eisenstein

The miracle of the Franco-Norwegian production *La Bataille de l'eau lourde* [1948] is that everything in the film would seem implausible if it had not been made with the real-life heroes of the drama who, in the Cinema Rex, come up on stage at the end. This is further proof that fiction seems truer than truth and that, while fate may think wrongly, the same does not go for human beings. Hitler keeps his treasure but, on two occasions, instead of having to grapple with Fafner, the knights are confronted by an old concierge.

An old concierge protects the holy of holies, the distillation room. It is an old concierge — and, moreover, a Norwegian — who guards the ferry on which Hitler's treasure is to be taken away. In this way, three men can operate undisturbed, against all probability, in the midst of a swarm of SS men. Who would believe it? This is what we are shown. And, no doubt, we would be more convinced by a story that was untrue.

The way that Eisentstein operates in *Battleship Potemkin* is the reverse. He makes up the story and it becomes even more moving and striking because of the splendid details he invents.

He invented the Odessa Steps. He invented the tarpaulin that their comrades threw over the sailors who were about to be shot. He invented the procession of people in front of the body.

Little by little, stills from the film were hung on the walls of the Ministry of War. At first they were labelled: 'Eistenstein's film'. Then, later: 'The *Potemkin* film'. Finally they became documentary shots of the naval uprising.

I was very close to Eisenstein after *Potemkin*. I admired him. He showed me the early work on *The General Line* and told me some good stories about it.

Here is one: while they were shooting, Eisenstein and his crew went into an *isba* in a lonely village. Above the bed, to their great surprise, they found two colour postcards. One

showed the Eiffel Tower, the other Cléo de Mérode. When
they asked the old peasant woman about them, she replied:
'It's the Emperor and the Empress.' For her, at the height of
Bolshevism, a colour portrait in which her eyes could
perceive nothing, could only represent the Tsar or the
Tsarina.

Here is another: the peasants thought that the camera was
photographing the women naked through their dresses.
They threatened the crew with pitchforks. They also thought
that the gloves the film-makers had been instructed to wear
as a protection against leprosy, concealed claws and devils'
feet.

Eisenstein would tell a mass of astonishing anecdotes, his
large body racked with laughter. He saw everything, heard
everything, registered everything. And if he sometimes
embroidered the truth, he never lied. It was to make it
stronger and more legible.

When they showed *Potemkin* in Monte Carlo, a former
sailor from the ship's crew, who was there, wrote to Eisen-
stein: 'Dear Mr Eisenstein, I have just seen myself in your
film. I was one of the sailors under the tarpaulin.' Yet
Eisenstein had entirely invented the tarpaulin. His genius
had taken the place of the man's memory.

In Eisenstein's presence, I often had proof of this victory of
imagination over facts. There was much evidence of the
same in the mechanics of his masterpiece, *Que Viva Mexico*.

Unfortunately, few people have seen this triumph of
cinematography. The film that is shown, is made up of
out-takes from the original: this means that the shots Eisen-
stein threw in the waste-paper basket exhibit a prodigious
wealth.

We were due to make a film together in Marseille. The
project was delayed by his trip to America, and we never
managed to agree on a date. Often, I close my eyes and
watch our ghost film, and feel Eisenstein's great body beside
me, shaking with laughter. [*Carrefour*, N° 179, February 18,
1948. Repeating the story of the tarpaulin in *Battleship
Potemkin*, in his *Journal d' un inconnu*, Cocteau notes: 'One

constantly discovers that myth takes the place of reality, that it is the cake into which our daily bread is transformed. It would be useless to predict how, by what tortuous path, or digestive tract; what rises or what collapses. Whoever set out to invent a myth and convince people of it, would be mad indeed.' Paris, Grasset, 1953, p. 141].

Jean Epstein

In the realm of the arts, I have always preferred the accidental to whatever follows the safe road — by which I mean accidents that are caused and controlled.

There are accidental men whom death fastens in eternal youth because they fought against custom. Today we are paying tribute to Jean Epstein, who was born in Warsaw in 1897 and died in Paris in 1953. Like Vigo, whose theme in *L'Atalante* he predated with *La Belle Nivernaise* in 1923, the author of *Coeur fidèle* did not seek success with the masses, he disconcerted them. Cinematography was his means of expression and, like a poet, he tried to bring the darkness within him into the light.

At this festival of Cannes, where it seems to me that technical progress predominates over the surprises that come from productive maladroitness, this homage to Epstein is significant. Colour, depth and other inventions, while in no way altering the laws of genius, will probably force young film-makers to stumble, grope and search, to find first and look afterwards (as Picasso so aptly put it), in short, to start again on the bottom of the board at the tail of the longest snake[1], in what seems like a failure but, in the long run, might well be the very emblem of success.

From *Coeur fidèle* to *Les Bâtisseurs*, Jean Epstein's life was a

---

1   In fact, Cocteau refers to the death's head in the *jeu de l'oie*, a game similar to snakes and ladders. (Tr)

model of rebellion against the rules, relying only on strength of mind and of heart. His images and the rhythm of his work have aged so little, that we should be gratified were we to find such a rhythm today, and images of such elegance and strength.

Abel Gance will talk to you about Epstein's books. I leave this pleasure to him. The first thing you are going to see is a passage from *Robert Macaire*: it will be projected at 24 frames a second, which takes nothing away from the film. On the contrary, speed accentuates the effect of puppetry in the human figures: Epstein's direction already tended towards this. Apart from the skilful framing of the images, you will observe the rich contrasts: they are like the workings of a decorative centrepiece in solid silver.

A final salute to Jean Epstein, and to Langlois, the dragon who guards his treasures. [*Cahiers du cinéma*, N° 24, June, 1953].

Joë Hamman

Some time ago, in a posthumous tribute to Gary Cooper, television showed the film where he describes the heroic age of the Far West, with period pictures chosen by him.

These old images, which predate cinematography, become more significant in their sculptural immobility than when they were put in motion by the film-makers whom they inspired.

What is striking in these still pictures, is always the savage nobility in the faces and attitudes of the figures: faces and attitudes with a savage beauty that predominates over the stigmata of crime.

This mysterious beauty comes from the fact that both men and women, whether young or old, were illuminated by the will to make their fortunes or, rather, to tear themselves away from the urban underworld.

In our age, which is weary, indifferent and seeks to

overcome the tedium of life by escaping to other worlds, this film seems astonishing in its dramatic freshness: the drama of ambitious souls which are confined to the human realm and have not yet considered devoting their energies to the service of an extraterrestrial ideal.

It seems to me that the figure of Joë Hamman sums up the daring of those hordes, whose splendid characters were presented to us by Gary Cooper.

Little by little, the relentless determination of the search for gold hidden beneath the earth, takes the place of the search itself and shapes the human gold of a wandering race whose unforgettable features are preserved in a few artless photographs.

I understand that in children's literature, caravans, locomotives, horses, firearms, arrows and cartridge belts sell better than science fiction and give more nourishment to childhood dreams than spaceship pilots.

Despite my tendency to believe that poetry is the pinnacle of science, I am consoled to learn that machines and robots stimulate the imagination of young people less than Indian head-dresses and the stampedes of *The Gold Rush*.

If we are to find another planet which has suffered the accident we call life, we must travel beyond our solar system, which is alas populated by future worlds or dead ones.

This leaves us time to listen to a man fascinated by the courage of adventurers whom we shall consider naïve, until such time as the future confronts us with the shock of our own present naïvety.

The secret of infinity is that there is no secret, or at least, that it is a secret only to the extent that we consider as progress our search to comprehend a mechanism that will remain eternally beyond our comprehension.

Let us recognize in Joë Hamman an active poet and a storyteller who is able to live out his stories. [Preface to Joë Hamman's book *Du Far West à Montmartre*, Paris, Editeurs Français Réunis, 1962].

Laurel and Hardy

Poor Villefranche! How can its stubborn poetry, or the
exquisite elegance of the English fleet anchored beneath my
light balcony of marble and iron, touch souls that have been
moulded by the elections and by Laurel and Hardy? Not that
I despise Laurel and Hardy. I love them. They are children
at play. There are times when their slapstick is rent with
uncontrollable lyricism and collapses into heaven and death.
I doubt whether the audience here in the unassuming rue du
Poilu, ready to laugh at the least sign of nobility or suffering,
can appreciate the magic charm of these two American
clowns. It appreciates pratfalls, flying dishes, saucepans on
the head and buckets of cold water — period. [*Paris-Soir*,
August 6, 1935].

Marcel Marceau

The stylistic exercise that you are about to see consists in
translating one silence by another. Through the wan charm
that he has inherited from Debureau and from Japanese
theatre, Marcel Marceau imitates the deceptive silence of
fish and flowers. He mysteriously evokes that vegetable life
which, in speeded-up films, is shown to be as rich in gesture
as the life of men. In short, he speaks.
    A mime breaks through the barrier of language; Paul
Paviot introduces us to 'Bip', the charming character
invented by Marceau.
    This character comes among us on tiptoe like a burglar,
with the terrifying presumption of moonlight. [Cover copy
for *Pantomimes*, by Paul Paviot, 1954].

Jean-Pierre Melville

Working with Jean-Pierre Melville was really a single compound of friendship in which the novel became a film, an Ariadne's reel unwinding until eventually it reached the Minotaur. I think that the book of *Les Enfants terribles* entered Melville without a hitch, as though he were its author.

Our arguments were those of true friends and I am sometimes sad that the turmoil of Paris has kept us apart from one another.

June 28, 1963. [In *Jean-Pierre Melville*, by Jean Wagner, Paris, Seghers, 1964].

Gérard Philipe

Prêté par la gloire.

What? Le Cid! What? The Prince of Homburg! What? All that glittering youth, amorous and victorious, yielded itself and was ensnared in the person of Gérard Philipe!

In a letter about Radiguet, Romain Rolland asked me: 'How could he let himself be vanquished by death after having dug his claws so deep into life?'

How could he let himself be vanquished, our brave Gérard, whose noble trajectory was like a bow, and why does this bow set such an arrow in our hearts?

There is a great mystery that no one can unravel, except in the image of the phoenix which, from one century to the next, immolates itself to be reborn; or else by the fables of the Greek sphinx or the Cretan Minotaur, which demand that the youngest and loveliest should be sacrificed to them.

We should fear prodigies.

All the same, it is hard to admit that such good fortune was necessarily short, and one would like to curse fate and to cry: 'Maldonne!' [November 26, 1959: *Les Lettres françaises*, N° 801, December 3, 1959].

Like Jean Marais, Gérard Philipe was the model of a flawless tragic actor.

Film obliged writers to find actors who were the same age as the characters they played: real Tristans, real Romeos, adolescent Yseults and Juliets. In the theatre, this led to a demand from audiences which could not be fulfilled, since young players who had to carry the roles of heroes and heroines did not have the strong shoulders of those actors who were never required to be the same age as in the story, but only the talent to make believe that they were.

With no actors to call on, the Cartel substitutes directors, costumes and sets.

Historically, it was Jean Marais, admonished by my memories of Mounet-Sully, Lucien Guitry and Edouard de Max, who first dared in *Les Parents terribles* to break away from that reserve which is essential on screen, but fatal on stage.

With Marais, Gérard Philipe thrust aside the rules of cinematography which had deprived the theatre of its great leads, so that in *Caligula* and *Le Cid* we saw him combine the ardour of his youth with a mysterious wisdom with which he seemed to have been endowed by some good fairy.

All the fairies were at his cradle. But one should always beware of the last among them, and Gérard's, following the others, told him: 'Your fame will be brief.' She was wrong: the good fairies have some nice tricks to play and their answer to this threat was: 'We shall ensure that your brief fame will be powerful enough to last a long time.'

It is a fact that the celebrated giants of the theatre, the caryatids supporting the temple, the Mounets and the Sarah Bernhardts, the Réjanes and the Guitrys, would not have survived a few weeks of the life that the taxman, cinema, radio and television impose on our young stars.

It is a fact that these giants exerted themselves very little: they luxuriated on bearskins or lounged on the terraces of boulevard cafés; it is also a fact that the pace of modern life tries the nerves of young actors and that the ease with which they support their very demanding parts is bought at the price of extreme exhaustion. But Gérard Philipe led a calm life and, while the repertory of the Théâtre National Populaire was harsh, he knew how to relax in the country and accept the fine and unblemished affection of the wife whom he adored.

No. Just as Raymond Radiguet, exalting and anticipating the good fortune of growing old, poured out his genius and emptied his coffers at a dizzying rate, so Gérard Philipe expended his spiritual wealth without counting the cost and dispensed his heart to the point of bankruptcy.

And what splendours emerged from the treasure-house so generously lavished upon us!

On the evening of *Le Cid*, after casting his riches across the theatre, you would have thought he was casting himself after them: this is how I understand the way that he came down into the audience at the end of his monologue.

It remains an unforgettable moment, comparable for me to the one when Jean Marais, lying flat on his face in the wings at the Théâtre des Ambassadeurs, waited for the tears to well up from the depths of Michel's being.

And this is why I offer the ears of the audience to these two splendid matadors of the theatre. [*Spectacle*, N° 1, 1960].

François Reichenbach

The Cannes Festival involves several degrees of success. There is delayed success, critical success, success with the public and success with the jury, which crowns the rest. François Reichenbach's admirable film [*L'Amérique insolite*, 1960] won the first round, but had still to conquer the final obstacle, which is not easy — and I say this as someone who knows, since I was several times president of the jury before being granted the platonic title of Honorary President at the Festival.

I imagine Reichenbach was the victim of a phenomenon which I understand, since I have suffered from it myself: that of casting a glance on the world (Saint-Simon would say, striking it with a glance) which upsets habits and shows things from an acute angle, easily confused with accusation and criticism. The same applies to those painters who daringly border on a style which is close to caricature, though never falling into it, and who only cease to astonish us in the long term. Van Gogh, Cézanne and Toulouse-Lautrec were called caricaturists, and Picasso is still considered something of a clown by the uneducated. For, strange though it may seem, I occasionally hear it said that I am playing a joke on people and that it would be naïve of anyone to take certain of my works seriously. These fine fools do not ask themselves what profit an artist might gain from such mystification, or why he should ruin his spiritual health for no good reason, dishonouring his muse and his priestly calling.

However, the absurd cost of a film condemns it to instant success and to break with the law of the muses, which requires us to wait for people's minds to become accustomed to what Baudelaire called 'the most recent expression of beauty', and to that which assaults their laziness.

I was not at Cannes on the evenings when they showed *L'Avventura*, *Virgin Spring* and *Moderato cantabile*: I have been told that the attitude of the invited audiences was so shameful that I agree with Lo Duca's remark in Maurice Bessy's paper, when he says that they should have been reprimanded. If I had been there, I should not have hesitated to do so.

On the other hand, there was no outcry over Reichenbach's film, which I did see. The audience only saw the passion with which our young tourist runs his third eye over a people in love with extremes and immune to that sense of the ridiculous which paralyzes civilized societies: Voltaire considered that, by becoming too intelligent, they had lost the ability to put out new shoots.

In the procession of contrasts that the film displays before us, there are only blades that crash, clash and suggest the dazzling choreography of the Hoffmann Girls' duel.

It would be crazy to mistake this joyful fencing for an armed assault, and I wonder what devilish trick allowed my dear friend Simenon to be taken in, since he is past master in the art of transcending what is mediocre and of unearthing treasures.

Admittedly, I was not sitting at the judges' table: it is easy to judge the judges, and while I think that the festival ought to help new works, it is equally useful for it to give the seal of approval to ones that are already successful.

It is the jury's business if it agrees unanimously to prefer some films and dismiss others. I am just surprised if the reason for the failure of Reichenbach's film (I mean, failure in the awards), is the one reported to me.

In that case, I submit in evidence the preamble that I recorded, of which only one passage remains. This proves my good faith and shows that my case for the defence is not a last-minute manoeuvre. [*Arts*, Nº 776, May 25, 1962].

Jean Renoir

I have the good fortune to possess, in my bedroom in the country, one of those little paintings by Renoir in which Jean is poking out his tongue over his school work. And, whenever I see a film by Jean Renoir or one of his plays (in fact, I only know one of them), I admire his fidelity to this image, protecting his child's heart and wrapping it up in the iridescence of a fruit in the sun.

If there is any family relationship between us, it is in the way that we choose the actors in a film far more because of their spiritual style than their physical appeal.

PS. Black-and-white films have colours too. [*Cahiers du cinéma*, Nº 82, April 1958].

It would be odd for a son of Renoir to be content merely to play with ghosts, even if colour adds the appearance of life.

I suppose Jean Renoir needed *a flesh-and-blood spectacle*. In any case, at a recent meeting of film-makers, he confided to me his secret passion for the stage.

In my bedroom in the country I have several paintings that were detached from a series which, I learned from Matisse, Renoir used magically to clean his brushes on at the end of his day's work.

I am looking at them now. Jean, with hair down to his shoulders and apple cheeks, is leaning over a desk and poking out the end of his tongue.

He is starting to write his play, that's for sure. And I wonder if his admirable work in film was not merely a holiday task.

So I greet the child and the man, and offer them my heartfelt good wishes. [Programme for *Orvet*, staged at the Théâtre de la Renaissance, March 3, 1955].

Jiri Trnka

The first time I had the good fortune to meet this extraordinary man, it was in connection with his film from a story by Hans Christian Andersen, *The Emperor's Nightingale*. He asked me to write the script.

On the day of the private preview, I invited four or five friends and, after the film, I was given the puppet of the Emperor to hand round. At this point, I observed something astonishing: a sort of awesome respect came over my friends. They hardly dared touch that mysterious and magical figure, no longer either an actor or a puppet, but Trnka's very soul which had adopted this shape. You may imagine how terrible it is to handle a soul and pass it from hand to hand like a mere *objet d'art*.

For a long time the little emperor lived in my room at the Palais-Royal. But, from being the Emperor of China, he became the Emperor of Siam, because of my siamese cats. They played with him, licked him and caressed him so much that little by little he disappeared. In the end, he reverted to what he should never have ceased to be: a disembodied soul returning to its origins, that is to say, mingled with Trnka's, so that he could once more give it flesh and invent a new form and new adventures for it.

Bit by bit, Trnka managed to suppress, oil out and link together the jerkiness between the innumerable gestures through which his patience and that of his team appeared to steal from nature the secret of life.

There is something truly wonderful about these films in which Trnka discovers a real unreality, instead of the commonplace human animals of cartoons. Nothing in his work is ever caricature and its nobility lies in making possible what in childhood we tried to believe possible by the sole power of the imagination.

All children animate their dolls and secretly make them live — and here we have a magician whose spells bring the dreams of childhood into existence.

Yesterday evening, we saw in Truffaut's film the miracle by which Jean-Pierre [Léaud] artlessly succeeds in a *tour de force* which the most talented actor could not hope to achieve. His interview with the psychiatrist is like a black team playing basketball, when people say: 'Yes, but it's not sport'; or a conjuror doing a card trick of whom they might say: 'Yes, but he's cheating'. In short, a strange gift raised him above the level of technique and allowed him to score on every throw.

This privilege is the same as the poetry which all children possess and which adults lose, unless they are careless enough to reserve a shadowy corner for it.

Trnka's is the realm of childhood and poetry, that Eden from which the demands of life sadly drive us daily further and further away.

Join me, if you will, in thanking him for allowing us to believe that the Guardian Angel has not closed the gates against us for ever. [*Les Lettres françaises*, N° 773, May 14, 1959].

Orson Welles

I met Orson Welles in 1936 at the end of my world tour. It
was in Harlem, at *Macbeth* played by a black cast, a strange
and splendid performance to which I was taken by Glenway
Westcott and Monroe Wheeler. Orson Welles was a very
young man. *Macbeth* brought us together again at the Venice
Festival in 1948. Oddly enough, I made no connection
between the young man of the black *Macbeth* and the famous
director who was going to show me another *Macbeth* (his
film) in a little theatre on the Lido. He it was who reminded
me, in a Venetian bar, that I had pointed out to him on the
previous occasion that the sleepwalking scene is usually
glossed over on stage, whereas I consider it to be crucial.

Orson Welles's *Macbeth* is a *film maudit*, in the noble sense
of the phrase which we used to promote the Biarritz Festival.

Orson Welles's *Macbeth* leaves its audience blind and deaf,
and I would guess that those who like it — among them
myself — are quite few. Welles shot the film very quickly
after many rehersals. This means that he wanted to keep the
same style as in the theatre, trying to prove that cinematog-
raphy can put any work under its magnifying-glass and
ignore what is supposed to be a cinematographic style. I
disapprove of the abbreviation 'cinema' because of what it
represents. At Venice you heard people constantly repeating
the same phrase: 'It's good cinema' or 'It's not good cinema'.
They even went on to say: 'This is a good film, but it's not
good cinema' or 'This one isn't a good film, but it's good
cinema'. We used to laugh at that, as you may imagine, and
when we were interviewed together on the radio, Welles and
I replied that we should be delighted to know what was a
'good cinema' film, and asked nothing better than to learn
the recipe so that we could follow it.

Orson Welles's *Macbeth* is a work of casual and savage
power. Wearing horns and cardboard crowns, dressed in
animal skins like the drivers of the first motor cars, the
heroes of the play move down the corridors of a kind of

dreamlike underground railway, in ruined cellars oozing moisture and through an abandoned coalmine. Not a single shot is left to chance. The camera is always at the spot from which the eye of destiny would choose to follow its victims. At times, we wonder in what era this nightmare is unfolding and, when we see Lady Macbeth for the first time, before the camera pulls back to establish where she is, we almost see her as a lady in a modern dress lying on a fur divan beside her telephone.

Orson Welles brings the talent of a considerable tragic actor to the role of *Macbeth* and, while a Scottish accent imitated by an American may be intolerable to English-speaking ears, I must admit that it did not bother me, and that it would not have done so even if I was perfectly fluent in English, because it is only to be expected that these strange monsters should speak a monstrous tongue in which the words of Shakespeare are still his words.

In short, I am a poor judge and a better judge than others, in the sense that, with nothing to impede my appreciation, I was entirely involved in the plot and my discomfort came from it, and not from any fault of pronunciation.

Welles took the film out of competition at Venice and it was shown by *Objectif 49* in 1949, in the Salle de la Chimie: everywhere it meets the same opposition. It is the epitome of Orson Welles, a character who despises custom and achieves success only through his weaknesses, which the audience latches onto like a lifebelt. Sometimes his audacity is so happily inspired and born under such a lucky star that the public allows itself to be won over — as, for example, in the scene from *Citizen Kane* where Kane breaks everything in his room, or the hall of mirrors in *The Lady from Shanghai*.

However, the fact is that after the syncopated rhythm of *Citizen Kane*, the audience expected a succession of syncopations and was disappointed by the calm beauty of *The Magnificent Ambersons*. It was not so easy to follow attentively the half-tones, the ins-and-outs that led us from the extraordinary image of the little millionaire, like Louis XIV, to his aunt's hysterical outburst.

What shocked fans of jazz and the jitterbug was the Welles
who took an interest in Balzac, Welles the psychologist,
Welles rebuilding American colonial homes. They rediscov-
ered Welles with his rather confused *Lady from Shanghai*, but
lost him again with *The Stranger*, and this switchback took us
down to the time when Orson Welles left Rome to come and
live in Paris.

He is a species of giant with a childlike gaze, a tree
crowded with birds and shade, a dog that has broken its
leash and gone to lie down in the flowerbed, an active idler, a
wise madman, a solitude hemmed in by the crowd, a student
asleep in class, a strategist who feigns drunkenness when he
wants to be left alone.

Better than anyone he seems to have adopted the noncha-
lant air of true strength, pretending to be completely adrift
and steering with a half-open eye. This derelict manner that
he sometimes affects, like a sleepy bear, protects him from
the cold and restless fever of the cinema world. It inspired
him to set sail, leave Hollywood and drift towards other
companions and other perspectives.

On the morning when I left Paris for New York, Orson
Welles sent me a clockwork toy, a splendid white rabbit that
wiggled its ears and beat a drum. It reminded me of the
drummer-rabbit that Apollinaire mentions in the preface
'Picasso-Matisse' to the Paul Guillaume exhibition which for
him stands for the surprise that greets us when we turn a
corner in the road.

This magnificent toy was Welles's real emblem, his genu-
ine signature; and when I get an Oscar from America
showing a woman on tiptoe, or when in France I am
presented with a little Victory of Samothrace, I consider
Orson Welles's white rabbit the Oscar of Oscars, and my
true prize.

The language of cinematography, I repeat, is not in words.
The first time I showed *Les Parents terribles* at the San Marco
cinema in Venice, on the fringe of the Festival from which I
should have followed his example with *Macbeth* and with-
drawn *L'Aigle à deux têtes*, we were sitting next to one another.

He cannot have fully understood the dialogue; but at the slightest nuance in the direction, he squeezed my arm as hard as he could. The screening was mediocre and, because there was not enough power in the projector, one could barely distinguish the faces, which are so important in a film of that kind. When I apologized for this, he told me that the beauty of a film is something that goes beyond the eyes and ears, residing neither in the dialogue nor in the projector — that it could be badly projected and inaudible, without destroying its rhythm.

I agree. At times in *The Magnificent Ambersons*, for example, he takes the idea to the point of finding an antidote to charm in unprepossessing photographic effects. But after seeing *Les Parents terribles*, in the Café Florian on the Piazza San Marco, we agreed that one should not go from one extreme of charm to the other and try to calculate the quality of patina in advance, since this would be the same as painting pictures that gave an immediate effect of ageing.

In fact, neither Welles nor I like to talk about our work. The spectacle of life gets in the way. We could stay motionless for a long time watching the bustle of the hotel around us. This immobility was very disconcerting to busy businessmen and anxious experts in cinematography. It was like the torture of the gondola when the busy businessmen and the anxious experts have to get into one and submit to its rhythm. People soon began to look askance at us. Our calm was seen as a form of espionage. Our silence was frightening and potentially explosive. If we happened to laugh, it was appalling. I have seen serious men hurry past us at full speed, fearful of somehow being tripped up. We were accused of the crime of '*lèse-festival*', on the grounds of forming a clique.

This was so unreal and so close to a form of collective psychosis that Welles and I could not manage to meet up in Paris.

He goes one way, I another. When he goes into a restaurant, the owner tells him that I have just left, and vice versa. We hate the telephone. In short, our meetings become what they ought to be: a miracle. And the miracle always happens when it has to.

I shall leave it to Bazin to tell you in detail about a many-sided body of work, which is not confined to cinematography, but in which journalism, the Martian landing joke, and his productions of *Julius Caesar* and *Around the World in 80 Days* have played a large part. I wanted to give a rapid portrait of a friend whom I love and admire, which is a pleonasm where Orson Welles is concerned, since my friendship and admiration are one and the same. [This text was the preface to André Bazin's essay on Orson Welles, published by P. A. Chavanne in 1950].

Whenever I think of Hans Christian Andersen's marvellous tale 'The Cave of the Winds', and the lines: 'The East wind entered. He was dressed as a Chinaman', I think of dear Orson as one of the sons, one of the winds visiting his mother's cave.

'The wind of New York entered. He was dressed as Orson Welles' — and this joyous and grave tempest blew, puffing away stupidity and routine.

The mistral makes me ill and stuns me, but 'Orson Welles' invigorates me and revitalizes my soul.

He is a bucket of hot and cold water for anyone who might be in danger of falling asleep.

Sacred monsters are a dying breed: one day their skeletons will be discovered and people will wonder what period they come from.

Orson is one of them, an exquisite and dangerous monster, a monster whom I love and to whose family I feel I belong. [*Les Lettres françaises*, N° 800, November 26, 1959].

Dear Orson Welles, how hard it is to survive when one is singular, in a plural world. We shall never speak Esperanto: that is a promise.

Je t'embrasse.

Milly, May 6, 1962. [*Cinéma 62*, N° 71, December 1962].

The violence and charm of Orson Welles makes him a poet. He never falls from the tightrope he walks above the cities and their dramas.

He is a poet, too, by virtue of the loyal friendship he brings to our dreams and our struggles.

Others will know, better than I, how to praise his work.

I shall be satisfied with sending him my fraternal greetings.

His is a firm handshake and I think of it whenever work forces me to overcome some obstacle. [In *Orson Welles* by Maurice Bessy, Paris, Seghers, 1963].

Robert Wiene

My dear Doctor,

You ask if there is a case for reviving your *Caligari* in another form. Certainly there is.

Caligari is not one of those works that take its place in the anthology of great exploits. We did not admire this film: it even irritated us in more ways than one. But — and this is better — we loved it and keep the memory of it inside us. Thus certain works circulate within us like magic blood and we were *charmed, enchanted, enraptured,* provided these words can regain their original meaning: charm being a deadly bond between beings, enchantment a sort of scourge that stuns everything and rapture a grasp that tears us out of ourselves.

Caligari, your first film, wonderfully sums up the singular era that is now displaying its death in the windows of department stores and on the hoardings of capital cities. But, as well as this, it had a look, a spirit, a breath, a '*Stimmung*' that go beyond the realm of mere fashion and preface the astonishing new era that is beginning, forebodings of which are recognizable to some of us by many signs. A hard era, cruel, bloody, austere, marked by pestilence and the stars, nightmares and revenge — an era of victims whose leaders, the initiated, will no longer be lightly chosen. An era as closed as a secret society which cannot be entered except with passwords and tests of endurance.

In short, not only do I approve of your intention to give your film a new life, but I actually advise you to do it, and will help you in whatever way I can.

My new play, *Les Chevaliers de la Table ronde*, requires the theatre to flare up with the same fire as burned when the stage was set up in the Middle Ages before a cathedral porch. It is a play about witchcraft and forebodings. Why should I not help you, as I am engaged in this, to broadcast on a similar wavelength? And why, whatever mild surprise this might cause in Parisian society, should I not accept the honour you do me in offering me the role of Cesare, the Sleepwalker, a poet's role, after all, since, if I am not mistaken, he walks over the roofs like moonlight and like moonlight goes into bedrooms and kills those who are sleeping there, under the influence of a malevolent force which controls him and takes advantage of his purity?

My dear Doctor, your film remains one of those very rare works that our understanding refuses to judge and that we accept fully and entirely. *Caligari* is *Caligari*. A new *Caligari* is essential. All the external details that weighed it down, the imbalance between the artificiality of the decor and the realism of the characters, its macabre and slightly superficial humour, will become the soul of the work.

Since then, you have proved that in your magician's hands an empty corridor with a curtain fluttering in the draught can be more disquieting than any ghost. Your *Caligari* of 1935 will be a prologue to the New Age, and I shall be proud to take an active part in it.

Good luck. [Jean Cocteau's reply to Robert Wiene, who had offered him the part played by Conrad Veidt, in a new version of *The Cabinet of Dr Caligari*. Published in *Paris-Midi*, December 1934].

Poetry and the Public

You wonder why you will never forget Marlene handing out tickets in Shanghai station or the astonishing manner in which Greta Garbo walked across the lobby in *Grand Hotel*. There is this mysterious poetry that emanates from a being and from a god, the intangible sex-appeal that the public looks for in a film, without even understanding the nature of its desires. At one time, Delluc, who died so young, tried to harness this unknown poetry, to make it perceptible to the whole audience. I am not talking about the films of Buñuel, or those of the writer of these lines; we were free and sought to do nothing more than lower the diving bell in which the Williamsons first went down into the sea, into the darkness of our human and inhuman depths. I want to tell you about those films (sadly, so few), in which the poetry captivates the audience without the use of the picturesque and without the use of old-fashioned techniques in the angle from which a scene is shot.

Feyder's *Le Grand jeu* is one such film, *Lac aux dames* another. Success has rewarded Feyder for his noble work. Now it is the turn of Marc Allégret's *Lac aux dames* to find a lasting place in our souls.

The main concern of a poet of the screen must, I feel, be to choose his actors in relation to the quality of freshness that they carry within them, since cinematography registers such hidden characteristics. It is impossible for an actor to overcome our disbelief under the pitiless lighting of a film, unless he is not content merely to capture movement, but also the forces that come from the inner being.

When you watch *Lac aux dames*, you do not believe for a moment that these actors could be replaced by any others. Like Georges Auric's music, which is so natural that one is tempted, unfairly, to think that it emerges quite spontaneously from the plot and the decor — in short, that it resembles the strange music that enters us in an express train, grandiose, mechanical, created by the rhythm of the

engine — like this (so to speak) 'inevitable' music, Simone
Simon, Rosine Deréan, Ila Meery, Jean-Pierre Aumont,
Michel Simon and Sokoloff seem inevitable as the interpret-
ers of a story that unfolds between them and moves us to the
extent that it spills over into nothing except the concerns that
drive them. Concerns with the moon and dreams, with
noctural sadness, with a fantom casino, a childhood attic, a
hypnotic power comparable to that which leaves us dis-
traught at the sight of the little paper body and exquisite
death's head of Katharine Hepburn. Yes: there is the same
lump in my throat and the same tears welling in my eyes as I
follow the actions of the scatter-brained Simone Simon and
the 'village idiot', Jean-Pierre Aumont, these two will-o'-the-
wisps, adoptive children of the spirits that inhabit the lake in
which they dive, swim, pass their time and drown, from
which they are resuscitated to live there in hiding under the
malevolent protection of the Erl-King. [*Oeuvres complètes*, Vol.
X, Lausanne, Marguerat, 1950].

The Origins of Films

Besides having the frivolous beauty of a casbah, Toulon is a
charming little provincial town. Its young people wear the
styles of the boutiques on the faubourg Saint-Denis and
think they are launching a fashion with the dances which
they can still be seen performing around the red platforms
put up for the 14th of July. In its cheap cinemas we are
obliged to sit through old films, which allows us to judge
them with hindsight and go back to their origins.

It was in Toulon, five years ago, that I had the good
fortune to discover a celebrated film that the so-called
Parisian 'élite' had advised me against seeing at the time.
This film, *Love Parade*, is a miraculous work by Lubitsch,
combining the fairy-tale magic of Hans Christian Andersen
with the brio of Strauss, not forgetting an extraordinary
couple of servants from a comic opera by Mozart. This year,

I have rediscovered a masterpiece, *Pépé le Moko*, in which Gabin elevates the type previously outlined by Préjean to an apotheosis. Our women far outshine the pale automata and illustrious ghosts of Hollywood. Their blazing cheeks and scarlet lips manage to overcome the half-tones of cinematography. Saturnin Fabre, though incidental to the plot, dominates it in the splendid character of the 'grandfather', and Fréhel, who threatened to hold up the story by doing his 'turn', is devastating: to what is already a slow and sticky strip of film, like a fly-paper, he adds a bluebottle, its wings and legs caught in an adhesive mixture of policemen, heat, solitude and Arab music.

Another fly-paper, even slower and more sticky: *Le Grand jeu*. When Gabin, in *Pépé le Moko*, crosses the labyrinth of the Casbah and decides to 'go down into the town', he has the same air as Pierre Richard-Willm drawn back to the fatal glue of the Legion. Did that style of Gabin's, which we see established as part of his screen character in *Quai des Brumes*, not originate with poor Delluc? *Fièvre* [1921] opened a bar door overlooking the port, vice and crime.

But while *Pépé le Moko* hits the jackpot without trying, with a sort of miraculous ease, *Quai des Brumes* is a masterpiece that has made up its mind to be one. Consequently, the film excites our admiration rather than our emotions. That vital and forceful actress, Mlle Michèle Morgan, is 'gretagarboized' by it.

Vital and forceful, because of her age and her debut, Mlle Luchaire is the reason why *Prison sans barreaux* [Léonide Moguy, 1938] may be even better than *Mädchen in Uniform*, the source of a whole family of films which seemed to have died of exhaustion with *Claudine* [Serge de Poligny, 1938].

Just remind me of the title of that silent film in which a girl and a boy in New York lose their way in the fairground on Coney Island and do not realize that they live next door to one another in the same appartment block. What a vein of freshness and youth! The second lucky streak for this youthful vein is surely *Drei von der Tankstelle* [W. Thiele, 1930] which is similar — and dissimilar — and which I have just seen again with real pleasure. The rhythm of *Drei von der Tankstelle* and its costumes almost take us back to the days of silent film, even though music plays a major role, so that we can witness the simple and joyful birth of all those American musicals, reaching perfection in those with Fred Astaire. This was the dawn of Charles Trenet, with his rural charm and his boater on the back of his head.

The game of origins. You can play it as you like in any town with little local cinemas. For example, I have just this minute come from seeing *La Danseuse de San Diego*, a first-class old film. It sums up the theme of comradeship victorious, in an endless succession of films. Origin: *A Girl in Every Port*.

Play the game and, without being jingoistic, you must agree that France has invented more than just the gramophone and photography. Many of our films — starting with those of Max Linder — led the way and, in 1938, the works of Gance, René Clair, Marc Allégret, Renoir, Dulac, Feyder and Duvivier astonish and revitalize the major international films. [*Ce soir*, July 5, 1938].

Continuation of a Retrospective

. . . Where was I? I am chattering on and talking about myself instead of about films. Oh, yes! I had just come away from *Tumultes* [Jean Boyer, 1931], with the observation that these films at the divide between silent cinema and the talkies express a different kind of energy from the films of today. In the case of *Tumultes*, the pungency may come from the fact that our actors and actresses were propelled into the technique of German cinema — with the result that they hardly knew where they were and could not profit in the slightest from the opportunities they were given. I am thinking of Miss Dietrich singing her famous lament from *The Blue Angel*, and I am astonished that Florelle lets the splendid song 'I belong to nobody' disintegrate into scraps and crumbs, when it should be at the centre of the film and set the tone. Despite this lacuna, there is, I repeat, a sombre power and an originality in the camerawork which, although it bears no relationship to the Russian method, enchants us and, through the eye, adjusts to the tempo of the heart. Need I add that an audience participates, and that, like the room where Dorian Gray first discovers Sybil Vane, plumbing silence to the point where it becomes a sort of shout in reverse, bursting with laughter or unrest, whistles or the stamping of feet, a confined space assists the fantom actors and resurrects them, raising them from the dead?

But already, in *Tumultes*, film-makers had ceased to use sound economically, as a precious commodity. It would be good to see the first talking pictures again.

Laziness, the child of habit, discourages one from creating a link between the ear and the eye, and exploiting it for gags and surprise effects. Remember: the laugh of bathing women . . . , the footsteps in pursuit through King Vidor's swamps . . . , the gunshot and the parting wagon . . . , the sound of the waves over the voice of Gary Cooper as he approaches with a girl in his arms . . . — haphazard examples — and so many other wonders, left behind by progress. [*Ce soir*, July 12, 1938].

End of a Retrospective

And now: *Ben-Hur*! And if the experience was painful, it was not the fault of the film, but of ourselves and the people we were twenty years ago. At that time, we were blinded by anti-Wagnerism, which made us devalue grandeur and the magnificence of bad taste.

What? Shall we take from this work — or, more precisely, from this undertaking — only the images that cannot go out of fashion? Keep the chariot race and the crumbling walls, and reject the scenes with the lepers and the Egyptian woman? That would be nibbling at the 'sacred monster' that

Ben-Hur brings to life before us, instead of devouring it whole. Quite probably, the type of women who attract us and the style of a star of 1938 will, in twenty years' time, take on a new kind of absurdity. What we should do is admire, from start to finish, a film whose audacity, power and nobility have never been equalled since.

Admittedly — leaving aside Ramon Novarro's beauty which is associated with the beauty of chariots or Roman galleys — his acting is close to the style of modern acting and makes the minor actors look old-fashioned. But this is because it burns with a brighter, higher and more intense flame, which finds expression in directness and simplicity. It is probable that, in the future, the inner fire of a screen actor or actress will soar above the restraint of others by its very excess and that Max's style will replace Antoine's, just as Antoine's replaced Mounet-Sully's. What I mean is that if Guitry were to be resurrected, without changing his rhythm, it is likely that his famous natural style would seem the least natural thing in the world. But at the time we were delighted by this false naturalness and only idiots would find it shocking.

Ben-Hur teaches an exemplary lesson. I remembered some rather odd leper women in a litter of pasteboard. In fact, the episode of the Hur women in the valley of the lepers and the scene where they come across Ben sleeping is superior (if that is possible) to the galloping white chariot that I once compared to a marble wind.

Progress means losing the dilettante's 'taste', that 'good taste' which corrupts the mind, constricts it and prevents it from expanding, so that we avert our eyes from an illustrious masterpiece, away from the Sphinx or the Acropolis.

The first lesson which effectively unblocked my eyes and my ears, was given me by Isadora Duncan. In Nice, when she was old and fat, she danced without the slightest coquetry. To begin with, her performance was embarassing. Then, age, weight and wrinkles vanished and only the spirit of the dance remained. This evening, in *Ben-Hur*, postcards and holy images from one's first communion were magnified by the director's sublime naïvety: the naïvety of a primitive painter; the same naïvety that built pyramids and temples with blocks of stone that our modern machinery would try to shift in vain.

Wagner's women, colossuses who run and shout with their hair flowing down their backs, and Siegfried, with a bird of prey on his head, coming down the hill towards the plump daughters of the Rhine, symbolize the theatre of the present day for me. When I was very young, they made me laugh. In the long run, one prefers to have epic stories and characters built to size.

Ben-Hur is the epic *par excellence*. [*Ce soir*, July 26, 1938].

Bonjour, Paris (Jean Image)

Paris is not protected by St Genevive alone. We must surely consider the Eiffel Tower a lightning conductor, designed to ward off certain kinds of thunderbolt.

As our guardian, the Eiffel Tower has an existence of his, or her own — male or female, according to whether myth makes it a sentinel or a saint. This film appears to strip off her crinoline and change her from citizeness to citizen: such things happen in our times.

So the Tower gets weary of staying in place on the banks of the Seine and we have a series of phenomena in which its dreams become actions through the marvellous power of cinematography and the imagination of an artist who bears the significant name: Image. [*Arts*, N° 435, October 29, 1953].

Le Diable au Corps (Claude Autant-Lara)

It is rare to sit in a chair and watch a story which you have lived through yourself, knowing the characters. I adopted

Radiguet like a son. Now, thanks to Claude
_____, Jean Aurenche, Pierre Bost and Michel
Kelber, and thanks to Micheline Presle and Gérard Philipe,
I was able to undergo a weird experience, comparable to a
dream. These fake characters and sets took the place of the
real characters and the real places, to the extent that I was
able to relive them without the slightest difficulty and with
profound emotion. I cannot express my gratitude for this
miracle. Claude Autant-Lara did not know the house in the
Parc Saint-Maur. He reconstructed it. The actors did not
know either Raymond or Marthe. They became them. They
became them to the point where I was lost in a labyrinth of
memories, and my soul was taken in by them. A journalist
from Bordeaux has said that the film is scandalous and ought
to be stopped. It has been taken off. The scandal is to have
banned a work that does honour to France and which no
nation except ours could have accomplished. I hope that
every cineast and every artist will protest against this
disgraceful act, which is a further symptom of our decline. It
is time that we faced up to our foolishness and overcame it.

France is a country of accidents and exceptions: it will
never be an assembly-line. Its workers only need to be lifted
up in a firm grasp, to show evidence of genius. *Le Diable au
corps* proves it. It is the model of an impossible undertaking
which has been made possible by the profound levity of a
first-class team. Nothing in it shocks me, and this is what
matters.

Alas, the day will come when journalists write: 'It is a
disgrace to show a colour film to mothers in mourning.'
There have always been killjoys in France, but France shines
in spite of them, thanks to the unique spirit of contradiction
and the need for anarchy that it enjoys. The book was
libelled as the film was libelled, proving that the film is
worthy of the book.

It is insane not to distinguish pollen-bearing insects from
Colorado beetles that devour plants. Critics, like us, are
subject to the laws for the propagation of the species. An
artist worried about art is like a flower reading a gardening

book. Nietszche points out that critics do not sting in order to wound us, but in order to live.

I congratulate the makers of the film *Le Diable au corps* for not having obeyed any of the rules of those who manufacture artifical flowers.

We love the characters, we love them for loving one another, and with them we hate war and mass hostility to happiness. [*La Revue du cinéma*, N° 7, Summer, 1947].

Jules et Jim (François Truffaut)

My dearest François,

I was well acquainted with the author of the book from which you took your film. He was the most sensitive and noble of men. In the film, I found nothing except delicacy of feeling and that charm of an era when leather jackets were white. [*L'Avant-Scène Cinéma*, N° 16, June 15, 1962].

Le Mystère Picasso (Henri-Georges Clouzot)

We know what Picasso said when he was asked: 'Why don't you go to New York? They would build you a golden bridge.' — 'And I would lie down on it.'

This is one of those well-aimed shots which he endlessly puts right on target, and it sums up the transcendental dandyism of a man who is a symbol of the impoverished magnificence of Spain: it reminds one of the University of Salamanca, at a time when Don Juan achieved sanctity through scandal. The students wore threadbare clothes, and gold chains around their necks, to prove that their rags were not a sign of poverty, but the height of elegance. This is the way that gypsies live and it is the style of a painter whose inspired creations pour forth like the water from a watering-

can and who clutters his homes with the sole furnishings of
his genius.

HAVE THOUGHT OF YOU ALL EVENING STOP
RAISE OUR GLASSES TO OUR FRIENDSHIP STOP
LOVE YOU AS YOU LOVE US. PABLO — GEORGES
— GEORGES. (The two Georges are Georges Clouzot and
Georges Auric whose contribution to the film seems to be a
sort of mysterious calligraphy for the ear).

Getting this telegram from Cannes demonstrates to me
once more that time is simply a perspective phenomenon,
that it does not exist in reality and that the heart still reigns
over a group in which Max Jacob and Apollinaire rejoice
beside us as they did in the Montparnasse of our youth.

One sunny Sunday morning Picasso and Clouzot showed
me their film. I shall never forget the great darkened theatre,
more full of light and life than the Croisette, in which Picasso
engaged in a bullfight with the void, the canvas, paper, ink
and the forces of inertia that are ranged in an unrelenting
stuggle against those who know how to conquer death.

Is not the sickness of our age that artists, who formerly
worked at *giving life*, now work to *forget life*?

There is nothing of the sort with Picasso, unless it is that
he tries to forget in an orgy of creation. If it rains in Cannes,
he is surprised at being told this: just as he rules over a world
of his own, in which he organizes errors until they cease to be
errors, in which objects and shapes obey him so that they
change form and take on the one he demands, so too he
invents his own climate, and the only storms, vagaries of
lightning, calm seas or skies are the ones he calls up in his
duel with the difficulty of being and the weariness of that
uninterrupted giving birth that Nietzsche means when he
speaks of 'men-mothers'.

Clouzot's film is an act of love. One guesses at the sweet
presence of holy women, seated in the wings and on a high
rostrum, and Auric accompanying a mass. Something sacred
emanates from the vast nocturnal nave in which Picasso
carries his own tiny light around, just as Michelangelo, when
he was painting the Sistine Chapel, wore a candle on his

forehead like the horn of a unicorn.

And here I am watching a mysterious documentary on the germination of human plants, lines and spots moving in accordance with a mechanism which, like that of flowers, must respond to something quite different from its appearance and the charm that is ascribed to it.

Picasso *plants* himself alive and *grows*. He sets his traps to catch certain insects and his scarecrows to ward off particular birds.

But I should not like to encroach upon the work of the critics. Since I am the phantom president, I wanted to respond to the telegram from my three friends and apologize for the circumstances that prevented me from taking my place in their box to offer a fraternal homage to their work. [*Les Lettres françaises*, N° 619, May 10, 1956].

Les Noces de Sable (André Zwobada)

A cine camera is the most indiscreet eye in the world, so the film-maker's art is a keyhole art. We have to surprise life through a keyhole.

A camera crew has just achieved a remarkable feat in Morocco. In his film, André Zwobada puts his eye to the keyhole of a place that has been blackened by exposure to the sun, a place that has neither keyholes nor doors: the desert.

He takes by surprise — and you might imagine that it is aware of being taken by surprise — this terrifying sea of pale sand in which the oases (the palm groves) are called ports.

All you who are accustomed to films with car chases, gunshots and crimes of passion: have the patience of spirits of sand.

Let this mysterious film slowly and surely enter your hearts.

Othello (Sergei Yutkevich)

My dear Sergei,

I had not, unfortunately, seen Orson Welles's *Othello* and I thank you for inviting me to your box at the Festival and fraternally showing me yours.

'Ten minutes, and ten years,' Whistler replied to the court in which he was accused of having spent too little time painting a portrait. And when I ask you how long it took to shoot your film, the reply was much the same: 'Six years, and six months'.

From the first minutes of a work in which the screen is invaded by hands, like creeping plants, you draw the Moor's great purple hand before our eyes and instruct us to forget Shakespeare's play, compelling us to see it as we have never seen it before.

So we proceed from one unknown to another and from surprise to surprise, even wondering whether Othello will kill Desdemona.

You seem to be dispensing the legacy of Eisenstein, who bequeathed you the secret of a slightly child-like, ordered wildness, a classical romanticism in the manner of Pushkin, a tale whose powerful realism puts it on the same plane as historical fact.

I am reminded of the sailor from the *Potemkin* who ended up in Monte Carlo and wrote to Eisenstein: 'I was one of the men under the tarpaulin', even though the episode of the tarpaulin is a pure invention.

Beside you, in the darkness, I should have liked to halt the projector and freeze the smallest gesture of your actors: praise dare not name them, except by the names of the characters that they portray.

And that Byzantine waterfront, those Cypriot forts, those Greek temples, where Othello, wearing the white toga of Oedipus, suddenly leaps into the snare of the gods.

And those waves that participate in the drama, wrapping Iago and his victim in their foam. And that labyrinth of fishing nets in which the unfortunate man expires, like the fish drumming against the bottom of the boat and dying, wrapped in rainbows.

And those red capes, the colour of anger. And those helmets, like cockfights. And, from one end to the other, the heraldic image of an eagle growing two heads and moving by slow degrees from the animal kingdom to the realm of heraldry.

This is indeed what your film unfolds. A dream that has escaped from sleep, a monster that has emerged from a dimension beyond any we know, a cyclone in which the calm epicentre is the look of that young wife, subject to her fate.

Yesterday evening, we saw Michèle Morgan achieve the miracle of portraying David's terrible puppet, and this evening I have returned to the Cap in company with the illustrious fantoms to whom you gave new life through a courageous transfusion of your heart's blood. [*Les Lettres françaises*, N° 618. May 3, 1956].

The Passion of Joan of Arc (Carl Dreyer)

Battleship Potemkin stirred us by pretending to be a documentary. *Joan of Arc* pretends to be a document from an age when there was no such thing as reportage. Dreyer seems to film through a system of telescopes, via a planet where the speed of light transmits the celebrated trial up to the year 1928 — a trial observed by a chair, a paving stone or a wooden beam, those witnesses to the dramas of history that touch us when we visit the places where they occurred. Carl Dreyer never uses a picturesque camera angle: he is a surveyor. Every one of his inspirations becomes legitimate; the heart is never distracted by the mind. Thus he achieves the feat of moving and intriguing us at the same time.

Falconetti, Silvain, Artaud . . . I dare not mention them: they act out, on a clean slate, their roles as the figures in this rapid calculation where the proof, by rule of thumb, is our

tears and those stunned people, unable to leave their seats. I
repeat, only one other film ever had such a profound effect on
me, and that was *Potemkin*. [Paris, Gallimard, 1928].

Pickpocket (Robert Bresson)

In making *Pickpocket*, Robert Bresson was inspired by one of
those gifts that would be a simple *tour de force*, were it not that
Mozart and Lulli have shown us how such apparent light-
ness of touch can be a means of expression for souls that are
both simple and profound. There is the occasion here for
misunderstanding and for the sort of confusion with idle play
that led to *Don Giovanni* being seen as a work to be listened to
with half an ear and Lulli as a fop at the beck and call of the
Prince.

Robert Bresson was absolutely right to choose Lulli to
accompany the ballet of pocket picking and the terrible
anxiety that accompanies the novice cutpurse. The acting
that he has managed to coax from a non-professional is
miraculous: not only does he bring long hands that might
belong to a pianist to the filching of wallets, but he has also
endowed his hero with the sort of existential terror of an
animal stalking its prey and fearful of being stalked in its
turn. A police trap saves the budding pickpocket and recalls
the poignant story of the murderer who returns every
evening to the scene of his crime, expecting to be arrested,
and faints with joy when he feels the handcuffs on his wrists.
Without the slightest artificiality in the plot, Robert Bresson
shows us the dizzying compulsion that drives the thief into
the lion's jaw, and the power of love that extricates him,
despite the bars of his cell.

I should imagine that all those who admired *Le Journal d'un
curé de campagne*, *Un condamné à mort s'est échappé* and *Les Dames
du bois de Boulogne* will hurry to applaud a ballet and a drama
that seems to have adopted Oliver Twist and Moll Flanders
as its godparents.

Jigokumon/Gate of Hell (Teinosuki Kinugasa)

In awarding the prize to *Jigokumon*, we did not imply that we were paying tribute to a tentative experiment, but to the marvellous cinematographic culmination of a centuries-old dramatic tradition. Plot, direction, actress, colour — everything in this film is miraculous. [Cannes Festival, 1954].

Le Sang Des Bêtes (Georges Franju)

Zola is a great poet and a great cineast. Few people question this. Although illustrious, he remains an outsider in his field. The locomotive expiring in the snow, the white horses at the mine, the girl emptying her pockets in the tunnel, the little boy bleeding under the popular genre prints and the drunkard on fire are all odd, cinematic images and their intensity, misunderstood, properly belongs in cinematography.

I thought of this when I saw M. Georges Franju's admirable documentary on the abattoirs. There is not a single shot that does not move us, almost for no cause, through the sole beauty of the style, the great visual calligraphy. Of course, the film is painful to watch: it will doubtless be accused of sadism because it seizes drama with both hands and never evades it. It shows us the sacrifice of innocent animals. At times, it rises to tragedy through the awful surprise that we feel in seeing gestures and attitudes that were previously unknown to us, and forcing us to confront them. The horse, struck on the forehead, which falls to its knees, already dead. The reflexes of decapitated calves, writhing and appearing to struggle. In short, a noble and ignoble world unfurling its last wave of blood across a white tablecloth, at which the gourmet need no longer consider the agony of the victims in whose flesh his fork is sunk.

Around the sacrificial table extends the town, made up of several towns and several villages, the town which one thought one knew but which one does not know, with its funereal marine sky above the quite unsuspected setting of the canal de l'Ourcq.

You will never forget the slow-moving barge, decked in linen, or the shrouds in the animals' morgue, which are composed of their own skins.

Once again, courageous film-makers, who take no account of success, prove that cinematography is a medium for realism and lyricism, and that everything depends on the angle from which one observes the spectacle of life — the angle from which they constrain us to share a singular vision of things and emphasize the everyday miracle that lies within them.

Une Si Jolie Petite Plage (Yves Allégret)

Une si jolie petite plage is one of the first French films to take a heroic stand against the fatal industrialization of cinematography. By the implacable unfolding of its design, by the photography in which Alekan's sheer science obliterates toil and by the high cage of rain where Gérard Philipe wonderfully exhibits the features of a wounded bird, Yves Allégret's film deserves an audience that will forget its preconceived ideas about film and read it like a book. [November 30, 1948]

Bicycle Thief (Vittorio De Sica)

A working man is broke. He is offered a job sticking bills. He needs a bicycle. His wife sells the bedlinen. He buys the bike, but it is stolen from him. This is the visual writing, with light as ink, of a lens registering the workings of the soul in a manner that can be compared to Gogol constructing a drama around a trivial anecdote. [*Paris-Presse*, August 26, 1949]

Les Yeux Sans Visage (Georges Franju)

It took a lot of courage to make such a film, and the almost monstruous calm of Pierre Brasseur and the elfin lightness of Mlle Scob to make it bearable.

But the horror film has a noble ancestry and Franju has not forgotten the golden rule, which is to apply the greatest possible realism to the depiction of the unreal.

The awful thing about *Les Yeux sans visage* is that we believe in it.

And what will be the punishment of this man who steals faces so that he can try to give one back to his daughter, so that through his sin this disfigured daughter can find a new face?

It is the dream of Jezabel, to lose one's own face through the workings of an appalling vengeance of fate.

The film's ancestors live in Germany, the Germany of the great cinematographic era of *Nosferatu*.

It has been a long time since we last experienced the dark poetry and the hypnotic effect of the macabre, the houses of doom and fabulous monsters of the screen.

As in his admirable *Le Sang des bêtes*, Franju does not tremble on the brink. He dives in. He leads us implacably on to the very limits of what our nerves can stand.

Hollywood

Q. *What do you feel about Hollywood? What do you think about American films today?*

A. Hollywood is a royal house exhausted by intermarriage.

Q. *Does American cinema have a beneficial effect, or does it hamper the development of world cinema production?*

A. It has no serious influence on important work, because that is created out of opposition. For example, the slowness of the montage in *Le Sang d'un poète* derived from the speed of American montage. The world of art progresses through its spirit of contradiction.

Q. *Have you, personally, been influenced by Hollywood in your work? If so, what directors and what films?*

A. Harry Langdon always amazed me (and, if I am not mistaken, ruined his producers).

Q. *Which recent American films have you found most interesting?*

A. I have been struck by the 16mm films that I am sent by young people who are looking for an opening for their work. [*Cahiers du cinéma*, N° 54, Christmas 1955]

Japanese Cinema

In our age, which is deprived of the ceremonial, nothing has impressed me more deeply than to learn that Japan is going back to the roots of its past. The Golden Dragon is still unwinding its coils. We see the emergence of sea monsters, and samurai like magnificent crustaceans. At the Cannes Festival, the Japanese told me: 'Come and make a film in our country. Our style is leaning towards the West. Your film will be Japanese.' I was greatly touched by this notion of distance and perspective. A week of French films can only strengthen the link between our apparently contradictory impulses. We are bound together by a comparable sense of humanity, drama, mystery, modest elegance, precise forms and that simplicity which derives from complexity. What is style? Saying complicated things in a simple way. And while a barbarous style consists in complicating what is simple, no one employs the former method better than you. I love you and greet your island in which there is no hiding place for vulgarity. The East's only mistake was an excess of modesty, underestimating its own wisdom and believing, alas, in ours. For my part, I bow respectfully to Prince Gengi who, observing the snow gliding across his sleeve, wondered at anything so lovely and, realising that he was alone, wept because he had no friend to tell about it. [*Unifrance Film*, N° 27, October-November, 1953]

The Myth of Woman

The Myth of Woman is all the more important in cinematography since women's roles almost always predominate over men's on the stage. But film petrifies, reminding me of what Mussorgsky said on his deathbed: 'One day, art will consist of talking statues.' When I was young, I saw young people waiting for Greta Garbo after *a film*, such was the power of her mythological presence. They were waiting at the same door of the Paramount (which is built on the site of the Vaudeville theatre).

Colour will modify the myth. The talking statues will become polychrome ones and closer to reality. They will lose some of their mystery.

Woman is more secretive than man and cinematography uncovers secrets. An eye is an open window on the soul. At times, I have become a friend to great film actresses. The contract of friendship was instantaneous. I knew them *through and through* and they knew me thanks to another woman: the Muse of Cinema whom the nine sisters have accepted into their close and strict circle.

Physical charms can create a vast realm of love, but that counts for little. It is the individual spirit of the actress that eventually wins through.

My only sorrow is that the thunderous advance of cinematography may prevent the young from experiencing the myth of the great ghosts who are vanishing from the theatre and whom we hope to see live again thanks to the resurrectionist device of film. [*Cahiers du cinéma*, N° 30, Christmas 1953]

Actors

In real life, Diderot was very skilful at feigning emotions he did not feel: he could, at will, move himself to tears. Rousseau records the fact. It was doubtless having this great acting talent that made him believe in the theory of insincerity in actors, because we have a tendency to judge others according to ourselves. Yet, while there are some actors who are temperamentally unable to attain the truth except through falsehood, I know others who can only play from their innermost being and for whom any self-awareness would be disastrous: they absorb their characters until they lose themselves in them, to the point where they forget the outcome of the scene that they play evening after evening.

Anyone who subjects the spirited and enchanting milieu of the stage to a school or a method, knows very little about it.

You have to love actors as I do, to forgive all their weaknesses and study with the heart this astounding stable of thoroughbreds, understanding their pride and their mischief, to engage with a world of false perspectives in which you are liable to be lost unless you realize that they consider its proportions exact and plunge into it with a profound conviction that they are growing taller or smaller before our eyes. I might add that even those actors who subscribe to Diderot's paradox deceive us in perfect good faith and surpass themselves on the odd evening when their very being is intimately fused with the mechanics of their calculated deception.

Am I (as they say) a child of the boards? Probably. I have always adored the theatre and been infected with its red and gold rash. As soon as I cross the deck, the tackle and the cabins of that tempest-torn ship which are the wings of a theatre when the curtain is up, I feel the exquisite anguish of a Monte Carlo gambler. And I do not mean a theatre where one of my own plays is showing, but any theatre with any play — the only club that I would visit, given the time and choice.

Jouvet said to me the other day: 'Our profession is an atrocious one. It torments us in our dreams. Then the anxiety begins in the morning and lasts to the evening, when we have to make dead people live. We are insane!'

People who treat the players in an offhand way, who think they are enjoying themselves and startle them out of their hypnosis by coming in late to the theatre, should reflect on these words of a famous actor who is always considered calm and thought to have absolute control of his nerves.

Serge Lido and Dance

A balletomane is a very particular type, and I have seen some extraordinary examples. One was General Bezobrazow who followed Sergei Diaghilev's Ballet Russe, hanging around in the wings, and silently moving through the whirling mass of the corps de ballet, the Sylphides or Prince Igor's archers. Another is Serge Lido, although he is armed with a camera. Without the love that he feels for everything to do with dance, the camera would be useless. He would merely photograph. He would turn a feverish excitement to stone.

In the event, it is Lido's very heart that drives the camera hanging around his neck. Like the ghost of General Bezobrazow, Lido haunts the wings whenever our theatre rises to the level of magnificent gesticulation.

With a mixture of lens and soul, he obtains numerous images in which movement is plucked out of death. Sometimes the stills from a film are often more suggestive than the film itself. Sometimes Lido's photographs make us dream of a ballet in which human weight would be abolished and the proscenium arch become the glass wall of some fabulous aquarium. [*La Danse*, Paris, Masques, 1947].

The Genius of Our Workers

There are no such things as miracles. One performs them
and one deserves them. There are neither magicians nor
sorcerers, and these terms, which are constantly used in
referring to me, are incorrect. Everything comes down to
work and the intensity of concentration that you bring to it.

The weariness of work gives the worker a sort of slumber
that one lapses into on one's feet. This waking sleep makes
the public confuse what is produced by it with dreams.

Art is a shared dream. The artist does not describe his
dreams, he dreams in public. Consequently he needs an
audience that is capable of submitting to collective hypnosis
and of following his lead into sleep so that the realism of the
dream, encountering no opposition from their habitual state
of mind, can sink effortlessly into them.

This phenomenon is almost impossible to achieve in
France, where the mass is made up of individuals who resist
being absorbed, refusing to form a compound or to become a
single, permeable being.

It is also true that, in the field of cinematography, the
dream I mentioned would remain an individual one unless
there was a team: that is, a group of technicians and workers
who make the subjective objective and, in a sense, represent
a kind of archeological undertaking, a group of diggers who
help a man to bring something out of the darkness within
him — a darkness in which this something already exists and
from which it is released with delicate care.

Georges Clouzot says that there is no technique in cinema-
tography: according to him, there is only invention. And I
agree. But he is talking about our role as craftsmen-directors;
because you wonder what would become of the director's
imagination and inventions without technique, that is to say,
without the aid of technicians. Here again, we need to
change the usual terminology.

In reality, the work of cinematographic technicians can
also be ascribed to the imagination. I am always astonished

by the ingenuity of a handful of men who form one body with their chief and become his hands and his soul. While the actors are the letters of our alphabet and become the style of a work written in images, the workers on the crew, who are sometimes quite unsophisticated men, understand what is wanted of them at a glance.

They make the impossible possible, in an instant. You can demand anything at all of them, and set them any problem. They will solve it. They never say no. They never sulk, never hang around, never raise an objection.

They think and they find. I might even say, borrowing a fine phrase from Picasso, that they find first and look afterwards. They find with lightning rapidity. Then, by their genius (and I emphasize the word), they make up for the deficiencies of our material.

Either the studio provides nothing except a dusty hangar with none of the machinery that might make our work simpler — or, if it does have the machinery, it can't be used — or else we take our crew off to real locations where they instantly have to hang up the lights, nail the scenery and lay down tracks without damaging anything, to invent a mobile studio which must leave no trace behind after our departure.

People use the word 'genius' with too much restraint. It is not the sole prerogative of the Goethes and Shakespeares of this world. Genius extends through the whole range of humanity. Stendhal uses the word in referring to the exquisite ease with which some beings move and act.

In this sense, our workers have genius. I do not know if they provide a comparable service in foreign studios. What I do know is that, without that mystery of the beehive, our dreams as French writers would remain dreams and could never come to life in space and time.

For G. M. Film

I repeat what I have often said: that a film like *La Belle et la Bête* could never have been made without the affectionate collaboration of an entire team, from the leading star down to the most humble technician. Saint-Maurice is a veritable village where I like to live because its craftsmanship consists in giving form to our dreams. If my film is successful, I shall owe it to the craftsmen and technicians of G.M. Film's cinema laboratories, whose work is beyond praise. If it is not successful, I shall be consoled by the wonderful memory of that kindness, confidence, ingenuity, courage and family spirit that surrounded me and allowed me to achieve the impossible. The French film laboratories can be proud of themselves.

Nothing Good is Achieved Without Love . . .

Since I have been working on *La Belle et la Bête*, I have found that cinematography is a world like that of childhood, and I can see myself still in one of those sickrooms where I used to cut out pictures to make new pictures which I would stick into albums.

Even without realizing it, the author-director creates an atmosphere of collective hypnosis which is so powerful that the least technician finds the supernatural on which he is working quite natural and is surprised by nothing.

A merchant steals a rose from a Beast who, for this simple crime, condemns him to death. The Beast falls in love with the merchant's daughter and the daughter agrees to live with the Beast. The Beast is transformed into a fairy tale prince, and so on. The cameraman looks at all this, unperturbed, as if it were a realistic drama. Better still, he seeks to communicate it with us to the rest of the world and to invent the

Le sang d'un poète — Lee Miller

Filming *Le Sang d'un poète*

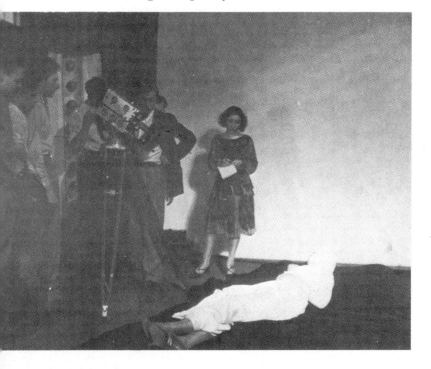

Le Sang d'un poète — Enrique Rivero

Le Sang d'un poète — Enrique Rivero (left) and Lee Miller (right)

Filming *L'Aigle à deux têtes* — Jean Cocteau (left)
and Yvonne de Bray (right)

L'Aigle à deux têtes — Jean Cocteau and Jean Marais

L'Aigle à deux têtes — Edwige Feuillère and Jean Marais

L'Aigle à deux têtes — Edwige Feuillère and Jean Marais

Les Parents terribles — Jean Marais

Les Parents terribles — Yvonne de Bray and Jean Marais

Les Parents terribles — Jean Marais, Josette Day and Marcel André

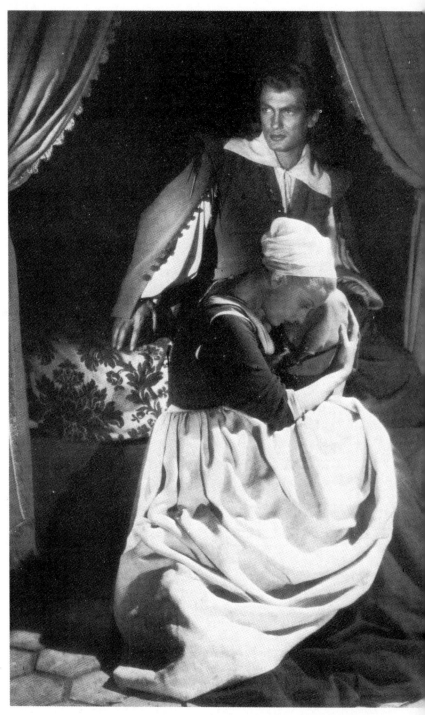

La Belle et la Bête — Josette Day and Jean Marais

Filming *Orphée* — Jean Cocteau (centre) and Marie Déa (standing, right)

Orphée — (from left to right) Jean Marais, Marie Déa
and François Périer

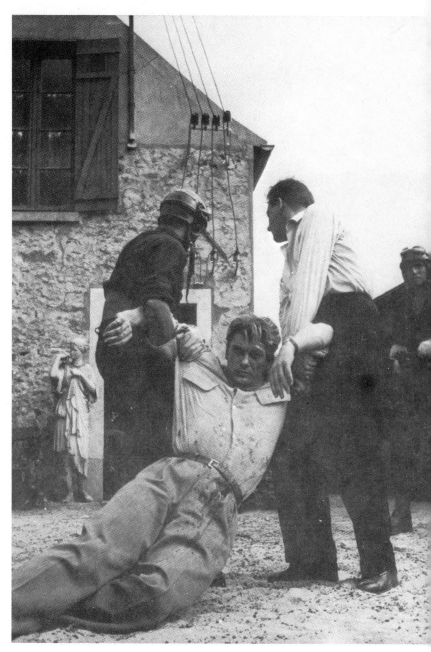

Orphée — Jean Marais

ming *L'Eternel retour* — Jean Marais, Jean Cocteau and Madeleine Sologne

L'Eternel retour — (from left to right) Jean Marais and Madeleine Sologne

Madeleine Sologne
and Jean Marais

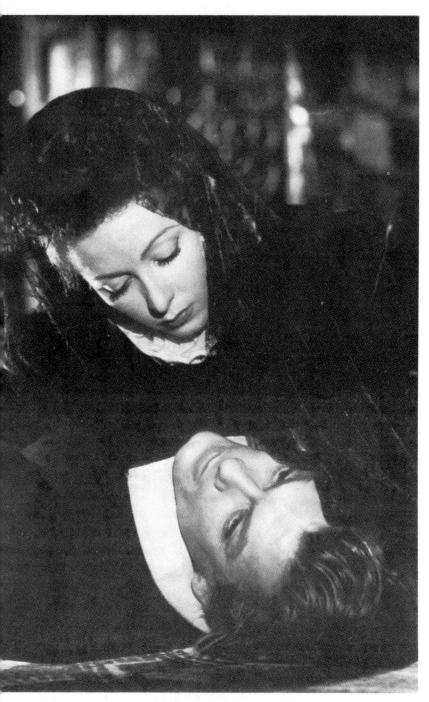

Ruy Blas — Danielle Darrieux and Jean Marais

Les Enfants terribles — Edouard Dermit, Renée Cosima
and Nicole Stéphane

Le Baron fantôme — Jean Cocteau

Le Testament d'Orphée — Jean Cocteau

Le Testament d'Orphée — Henri Crémieux (left)
and Jean Cocteau (right)

Jean Cocteau on the set of *Le Testament d'Orphée*

mechanism which will give form to a dream and make it an everyday occurrence.

I did not think it was possible, to this extent, to make up a team that could think with a single head and a single heart. So I observe, minute by minute, that the secret of cinematogaphy must be one's greater or lesser ability to bring together specialists who take to one another and are passionately committed to the same ends. The camera registers both the visible and the invisible, what you show it and what you do not. Whatever the talent and the money expended on a film, it will betray the ambiance of the team that makes it. A studio full of quarrels will coarsen it and weigh it down. A studio of friendship and mutual understanding will give it wings.

You cannot be too careful in preparing the ground. The chemical compound that you are mixing can quite rapidly become a deadly precipitate. Did you know that films have a resistance of their own and that this occult resistance of a work in its very being can create such peculiar obstacles that businessmen, who consider the art an industry, end by attributing them to fate?

Some molecules cannot live side-by-side or mix. The organism breaks down: the chief cameraman does not get his shots; the dolly leaves its mount; the actress falls ill; the lab scratches the film; and so on and so forth. In short, the backers complain of bad luck, when in fact it is just one of those freaks, of order or anarchy, that govern creative work.

This is one of the numberless phenomena peculiar to cinematography, an enigma that I am trying to solve, but which I think is insoluble without the x-ray of love.

PS These lines were written for *Ciné-Revue* and for my Belgian friends, to whom I should like, in every sense, to express my profound gratitude.

I sometimes think of Belgium while I work, and of the welcome that I always enjoy there, and how I can be worthy of it. [*Ciné-Revue*, N° 5, February 1, 1946].

III   Poésie de Cinéma

A cinema studio is a factory for making ghosts. The cinema is a ghost language that has to be learned. It is incredible for a poet to know this. The day when a director understands that the author's role is not limited to the script (to writing it) — the day when the author reveals himself — then the dead language of cinema will become a living language. [*Album du Cinéma*, 1943].

Le Sang d'un poète

Whether in the cinema or not, art has two faces. It is either active art, a sort of sublimated journalism, which aims to render some kind of service to society, or it is that art which is occult, hidden, a sort of explosive on a time-fuse, which at first seems like a scandalous luxury, but in the long run presents the least perishable face of a nation. Cinematography, that very secret form of art, usually very unpopular with the public outside the shadows (I mean those that conceal books with small circulations and plays in single performances), because of its inaccessibility and the ruinous costs it entails, and because it demands a huge and immediate recovery of these costs — cinematography, that weapon of poets *par excellence*, only rarely escapes being used in a way that it was fated to be used. There is no freedom in this realm of perfect freedom! And when great poets like Chaplin or Keaton employ it, their only excuse is to excite laughter. If they were to direct the same force towards drama and if their gags, instead of submitting to the demands of burlesque, were to serve the ends of tragedy, the laughter of the audience would soon become savage and mob violence take the place of applause.

Cinematography is moving further and further away from the motor car and trying to become like the theatre, a dismal, pseudo-theatre which no longer exploits the supernatural esperanto of the image.

Scenes like the one with the cow or the conductor in Buñuel's *L'Age d'or* may be thought of as a major event: the appearance of a tragic gag. I do not doubt that they will be greeted with malicious laughter; but they exist, none the less, and nothing will now halt the flow of the black river that pours from them.

This, then, is the true role of the patron. The patron is not there to support good business investments, but bad ones, some bad ones, the best there are, the long-term successes, the mysterious profits that are beyond the reach of dry little purses and remain the exclusive privilege of the truly rich: those who are rich in heart as well as in money.

This the fine example offered by the Vicomte and Vicomtesse de Noailles: a great name and a great fortune which do not seek the spotlights of fashion, but pass beyond them into the shadows where artists work, the ones that they love, recognize and applaud, who would not find the means to express themselves freely from any other source.

This is why I accepted their offer after so many refusals. Despite the affability of large firms, simple politeness obliges us not to make them run risks and to be prudent in the work we do for them. Here, there is no prudence. The shareholders shut their eyes, block their ears and are tactful enough not to trouble the work of the studio. The surprise will be a good one, whatever it is, even if it draws down the reproaches of fashionable society, in the midst of which our patrons, mocked, ridiculed and subjected to the worst insults, quite calmly return to a role which is unknown in smart salons and which can only ennoble them.

Le Sang d'un poète, a film in Chaplin's sense of the word, is a realistic documentary about unreal events. The style is more important than the plot and the style of the images allows everyone to suit himself and read the symbols as he wants: because Freud was right when he said, in the preface to *The Gambler*, that an artist does not need to have thought of certain things for them subsequently to become the main theme in his work. [*Le Figaro*, November 9, 1930].

La Belle et la Bête

I don't think there is any job which is more entertaining and less monotonous than a film director's. What is a director? After the work that I have done over the past few months, I have realized that he is a team. Our role consists in grouping, loving, interesting and keeping alive that flame without which the shots that make up the film would be merely ashes.

Sometimes, in the midst of that great contraption of light, pandemonium and anarchy, I wonder if it is I who am directing the work, or the work that is directing me, strangely accelerating down a steeper and steeper slope.

Clément, my right hand; Ibéria, the left; Alekan, the cameraman; Tiquet, his assistant; Lucile, my script girl; Bérard, who transforms the furniture and the costumes; Aldo, the photographer — all give me the feeling that they are set in motion by my nerves and my vibrations. Not to mention the actors, chiefly Josette Day and Jean Marais, whom I try to influence as little as possible, since the atmosphere that they absorb inspires them and prevents them from losing their way.

But what a struggle it is! A struggle against electricity and crackling arc lights; against the treacherous little illnesses brought on by fatigue; against running make-up, a sound system that records intrusive noises, the conscience of the chief cameraman who wants to adjust the lighting, the poor filmstock that will not register contrasts, and the lab which over- or under-exposes the film; a struggle, minute-by-minute, that exhausts you — because when the cameras are running, your heart stops between the word 'action' and the word 'cut'.

A film does not belong either to the past, or to the present, or to the future. It is confined to a time of its own, which is beyond analysis.

As far as dialogue is concerned, I think it should not play too large a part and that action can replace it to advantage.

But this restraint has to be guided by the internal rhythm of the story. In *Les dames du bois de Boulogne*, I was only the servant of Robert Bresson, who wanted the dialogue to be dry and close to the style of Diderot. His film was a modern film, so I had to convert the style and, unfortunately, retain few sentences from Diderot. The only line that was precisely reproduced was not Diderot's, but Pierre Reverdy's: it comes from a play that has not yet been staged — 'There is no such thing as love; there are only the proofs of love.' It figures in *Les dames du bois de Boulogne* as a tribute to a great poet and a great friend.

There is little talking in *La Belle et la Bête*. It is a fairy tale. The characters should seem to be described by the author, rather than describing themselves. Silence, music, wind and trailing dresses will complement the wonderful adventure that Mme Leprince de Beaumont added to Perrault's stories in the edition published in the Bibliothèque Rose.

France never gives sufficient acknowledgement to the astonishing assistance given us by the cameramen and lighting technicians in the cinema. These happy, serious, precious, speedy and airborne workers are our answer to the Hollywood electric organ. This needs to be understood and we should not, for example, treat our veritable orchestral conductors of sound as if they were mere mechanics.

The list of essential reforms is too long.

We shall just have to be like children, who know the secret of playing with makeshift toys in such a way that they become the finest toys in the world. [*Carrefour*, October 19, 1945].

I am not shocked by the numerous criticisms to which my film *La Belle et la Bête* has been subjected. I expected them. I am well used to it. Most of them derive from a lack of distancing and from the speed with which cinematography accustoms the eyes and ears to see and hear things offhandedly, when they demand deep concentration; and from the fact that the style of French legends has been forgotten. One of the more considered articles criticizes me for Jean Marais' triple part, so I ought to explain this.

This triple role illustrates the naïvety of the fairy world and why it now keeps apart from the human one. The fairies (who operate in my film beyond the edge of the screen) notice that Belle is attracted to Avenant, a young man who is unworthy of her. They think that Belle will love the Beast if

the Beast looks like Avenant. They think they are punishing
Avenant, who tries to kill the Beast, by giving him the other's
ugliness. They think they are rewarding the Beast and Belle
by giving him the beauty of Avenant with, additionally, the
Beast's nobility — and that this mixture will be the prince of
her dreams. Naïve fairies!

Like the girls of 1946 who have written to me after seeing
my film, Belle prefers the Beast to the prince. 'Are you
happy?' he asks her, and she replies: 'I shall have to get used
to it.'

But this marriage is possible because Avenant, the Beast
and the prince are one and the same. Otherwise Belle would
run away from the handsome stranger. A great mystery
combines the three men who approach her; without it, the
film would be merely a crude chapbook.

People refer to the slowness of the film. Yet, if cinematog-
raphy cannot encompass slowness, it is not an art. And yet it
is one. My slowness is not slowness, but rhythm. While I was
making the film, I continually hummed Lulli's minuet from
Le bourgeois gentilhomme to myself. Its gravity, its syncopa-
tions, its solemn individuality suggested a kind of sacred
terror, carrying me as far away in time as a documentary on
South African dance would do in space.

Critics ought not to think of cinematography solely as
entertainment: they should be able to go back to a film and
study it, if only, in the case of my own film, to discover
Georges Auric's sublime background music, to notice the
miracle of Josette Day's graceful movements and the
restrained grandeur with which Jean Marais expresses the
animal suffering of the smitten creature he plays. All this, as
well as the Molièresque style of the sisters, the balance
achieved between the members of this family, the new depth
of Alekan's images and several other things, has remained
beyond the grasp of those who ought to bear witness for the
defence before the indictment levelled against us for centu-
ries.

How is it that the real audience and the most simple hearts
can read all these secrets as in an open book and write about

them in numerous letters to us that would make a critic's reputation?

This is the audience that I address, to express my gratitude to it.

The actor has an awesome job which consists in abolishing his labours to give an appearance of facility. The greater an actor is, the more his work is blurred: the more he seems to live his role and to impose it, the less the audience realizes the enormous effort he is making. The theatre is one world, the stage another. These two worlds are separated by the footlights, flaming and mysterious as an Archangel's sword. When the performance ends, the red curtain forms an absolute barrier, which cuts off the waves of the receding audience, that casts no backward glance towards the storm-battered wings, full of technicians clinging to glorious ship-wrecks, tangled ropes, jumbled perspectives and capsized fantoms.

Backstage in the theatre, like the floor of a film studio, is not the pleasant place that one imagines, but a little factory in which emotions are gathered up and remade every evening. How much discipline there is! Every evening these admirable mediums will communicate their hypnosis to the theatre or the screen and give life to characters of shadow, ink and paper.

When I was writing *La Belle et la Bête*, I tried to make the film that I used to imagine — at a time when I was still too young to go to the cinema or the theatre — from my parents' mysterious outings and the programmes that they left in my room.

In *La Belle et la Bête*, as in *Les Parents terribles*, my only advice to Jean Marais was that, after reading his part, he should play it like those actors that he had never seen and try to have a mental image of their glamour. It is no doubt thanks to this method that he performs with such ardour and excess, at the extreme limit of his powers, and startles us by sharply breaking away from a 'modern' acting style. Of course, his success in my play and in my films is attributable to his own individual gifts, but these natural gifts are complemented by a desire to overcome old habits, to adopt the awkwardness of a clumsy animal and the savagery of a wild beast.

Many people thought that the parts fitted him, by allowing him to follow his natural bent. This is wrong. Nothing is harder for an actor than to interpret characters which resemble him. 'When I play a mother,' Réjane used to tell me, 'I have to forget that I am a mother and that I love my son and my daughter.' [*Pour Tous*, N° 15, July 23, 1946].

Paul Eluard said that, to understand my film, you have to love your dog more than your car. After that, there is not a lot to say. But since the film is problematic and I have read so many misconceptions about it, I have decided to offer a few explanations. French literature is very sick. It devours badly-translated American literature, which it cannot digest: the Americans would be very surprised to discover how we exalt works that Americans themselves consider minor and to which they attach little importance. We should not be too harsh, because the opposite often happens and foreigners may accept and naturalize French books that we ourselves do not hold in high regard.

Moreover, what attracts the snobs of today is the poor quality of translation in these American books, which appeals to an increasing tendency to read a text very fast and very superficially, only seeking out what is picturesque. Obviously, this notion of the picturesque does not operate in the same way from one country to another, and things which appear quite normal to us will seem extraordinary to foreigners. It is to this difference of viewpoint that I attribute the success, for example, of Westerns in France and Pagnol's *La Femme du boulanger* in America. I might add that in France, where young people no longer buy books (they are too expensive or too rare), a veritable chasm has opened up between yesterday and today: Naturalism, so painfully established in 1889 by the Goncourt brothers and by Antoine, ousted by Symbolism, Cubism, Dadaism and

finally Surrealism, has started to flourish once again in the
ruins, and a whole younger generation, unaware of this,
believes it is inventing a definitive art form, all the more
appealing since it requires less effort.

We have recently seen some quite peculiar examples of
this. To quote just one: the latest Italian films, despised in
Italy, charm us with their lyrical Naturalism, a kind that is
truer than truth; Rossellini's *Paisà* is the most typical.

It was because of *Paisà*, in my case, and *Le Sang d'un poète* in
Rossellini's, that we decided to collaborate and make *La Voix
humaine* with Mme Magnani admirably playing the single
role.

French cinema is going through a very strange crisis. At
one time, producers considered wit, and even poetry as a
means to make profits with our help. But our narrowing
distribution circuit and increases in costs, while the price of
cinema seats remained the same, gradually drove business-
men of the cinema to become patrons — reluctant and
ill-tempered ones, as you might expect.

Nowadays, any film that rises above the mean in style
cannot make a profit in France and, except in the case of a
few large-scale prestige projects, output will fail and studios
close down.

In addition to that, a poet faces a major difficulty in
cinematographic work because of the immediate returns that
cinematography demands.

A book can wait. A play can flop. But a film must appeal
to its audience, and it is essential to combine several forces
that allow us to repel and attract at one and the same time.
Novelty invariably upsets aesthetes, critics and the masses,
who have become accustomed to certain conventions
through laziness, and are roused from their slumbers in the
most brutal and unpleasant manner by the slightest depar-
ture from these formulae.

The only hope for a film is that the audience, less deaf and
blind than the critics, or I should say more childlike and
more ready to be won over, may not obey the veto handed
down by literary judges and, as happened with *La Belle et la*

Bête, will view with innocence and love what was hidden
from the intelligentsia of the capital by their blinkers.

In short, when I decided to make a film which would be a
fairy story, and chose the least magical of all fairy tales — by
which I mean the one that would take least advantage of the
opportunities provided by modern cinematographic tech-
niques — it goes without saying that I knew I would put
people's backs up because I was going against the grain and,
once more, rejecting fashion.

Instead of realism, I wanted to replace it with the stylized
and rather crude vision of characters from Molière (at the
start of the film); and, in place of what people usually
consider supernatural and poetic, I would adopt a kind of
realistic style, avoiding imprecision and effects of mist,
superimposition and other outmoded techniques.

The leitmotif of the work was to be the continuity of the
type that women pursue, without knowing it, while believing
that they are changing loves, and the naïvety of fairies (or
those who invent them), who imagine that this type is
perfected until it attains conventional beauty. My aim was to
make the Beast so human, so appealing, so superior to men,
that his transformation into Prince Charming was a terrible
disappointment for Belle, in a sense forcing her to accept a
marriage of reason and a future summed up in the last
sentence of a fairy story: 'and they had many children.'

So I had to let down my audience and Belle at the same
time, and I slyly persuaded my chief cameraman, Alekan, to
film Jean Marais, as the Prince, in a bland and insipid style
in order to carry it off. And we did.

There are any number of letters from women, girls and
children to me or to my leading actor, written in 1947,
complaining at this transformation and regretting the disap-
pearance of the poor Beast who would have appalled them at
the time when Mme Leprince de Beaumont wrote the story.

When Mme Leprince de Beaumont published *La Belle et la
Bête*, she was a poor schoolmistress in England, and I
imagine the story originally came from Scotland.

The Anglo-Saxons know how to handle terror and the

bizarre better than anyone; and it is often said, in England, that there were Lords, the eldest sons of great families and heirs to titles, who were monsters hidden in the chambers of some castle.

I have great hopes that the Americans will be able to understand this, for three reasons:

1. America is the land of Edgar Allen Poe, of secret societies, mystics and ghosts, where a splendid musical lyricism is an everyday matter.

2. Childhood is fresher there and better preserved in men's spirits than in France, where they deliberately set out to lose it, because they consider it a weakness.

3. The things that influence French literature from America are already old and outdated in America itself, and Americans are looking for something different from what amazes us, but no longer amazes them.

Broadly speaking, this is what drove me to an experiment that I shall not repeat, because an experiment should be unique; and I would again compare this one to the launching of a seed that falls on favourable or unfavourable ground and drifts where it will.

What you ought to hear is much more than a voice. It is the whole route that the voice has travelled, the whole dark route through the human organism, intricate as a French horn. In short, it should echo the sound of the heart and carry it to you, until it becomes audible and visible, as in my old film *Le Sang d'un poète* where the audience hears it fill the theatre and sees it lifting the hero's lapels in time with the beat.

For what this voice expresses is my great sadness at not being in Prague, my sadness at being somewhere else while it is speaking to you, my sadness at not being able to take Nezval, Hoffmeister and Kopesky by the hand, to shake their hands and let them know, by touch, how warmly I desired our meeting and how reluctantly I have to forego it because of my work. Work! This is the only excuse I can offer for my absence: this labour that belabours me, never leaves me, hands me its orders and doesn't give a fig for my wishes or my pleasures.

I have tried to convince it that Prague was a place of work and that I would visit the factories where cinematography manages to put our dreams into cans; I tried to tell it — this work — that the magnificence of your city would be the starting-point for new projects; but nothing can persuade this master whom we serve, who despises us and does not deign to listen.

I know that *La Belle et la Bête* is also my voice which you will hear and that, beyond the screen, I am the teller of the tale and that I wanted the characters only to act to the extent that they belong to the word. I am aware that you will understand that this film is the contrary of what is called cinematographic in style and only tries to express, at whatever cost, and slowly, as required by an attentive and fussy child, very simple actions, the poetry of which has no more to do with me than table-turning does with the craftsman who makes the table.

I realize that you will notice how I have been economical with words and that, if the film that I offer you goes beyond its own limitations, it does so thanks to the mystery of transfiguration.

In reality, what do naïve fairies — or those who invent them — think? Avenant is handsome, the Beast ugly. Avenant is a bad boy, the Beast a good beast. A mixture of the two will make Belle happy by means of a perfect being: Prince Charming. That is what the fairies think.

They are wrong, and I am sure that you will see how Belle perceived the eyes of the Beast in Avenant and loved the Beast; and how Prince Charming spoils the excitement, so she will have to start a family and, as the fairy tales say, have lots of children.

Since I was a child myself I have been fascinated by *La Belle et la Bête* which was next to Perrault's stories beneath the red and gold cover of the Bibliothèque Rose.

I found the supernatural quite natural, and still do. I made this film without any cunning. I had to be a Beast to describe the sufferings of a Beast, and it was this that earned me the fine praise of our poet Paul Eluard: 'To understand this film,' he said, 'you must love your dog more than your car.' This is not always the case in theatres when a film is at the start of its career: only afterwards does it meet minds which will take it up. This is why I regret not being with this film in Prague and watching it with a fresh eye, in the darkness, beside you.

André Paulvé, Emile Darbon, my actors, my crew (the same that made *La Bataille du rail*), my set designer Christian Bérard and my musician Georges Auric greet you.

And now, close the eyes of intelligence which prejudges, and open those of the heart which does not. Be carried away. I have a story to tell. [Recorded for the screening of *La Belle et la Bête* in Prague].

Dear Belgian friends,

You have a Beauty and you have a Beast. The Beauty is a little country girl disguised as a Princess. The Beast is a Prince Charming who has been transformed into a beast. You have a family which lives in a house done in the style of Vermeer. You have a sombre castle done in the style of Gustave Doré. You have invisible fairies who think that everything is simple because they can wave their wands, when in fact nothing is simple, least of all the hearts of simple young women who prefer adventure to a sensible marriage. You have the puzzle of a look which stays the same and will be elucidated in the beyond. You have Paul Eluard's answer, when he was asked what he thought of the film and replied: 'To understand this film you must love your dog more than your car.' You have people who judge works and who judge people. You have the author who tells his story, steps back, watches, listens and can no more change into something else than change into what he is. You have Jean Cocteau who has just been speaking to you, and greets you. [For the screening of *La Belle et la Bête* in Belgium on December 3, 1946].

Dear and honoured Mei Lan Fang,

I have always thought of the arts of theatre and film as a religion. And I consider you the high priest of this religion.

It is an extraordinary honour for me to speak through your mouth.

If I had not been born in France, China would be my homeland. I love and respect all the forces through which it expresses its soul. Although I sometimes have difficulty in understanding them, I divine them with my heart. In *La Belle et la Bête*, I often presented you as an example to our actors and tried to get them to achieve the rhythm at which you excel. Jean Marais' look when he suffers at being an animal is exactly that of the sacred monsters in your legends. Josette Day's gestures are those of a Princess from one of your prints. And if I am fortunate enough to please the Chinese public, I think I shall have achieved my ambition and be so proud that afterwards anything could happen to me. I should reply to those who attack me: what do I care? Through the mouth of Mei Lan Fang, I have saluted the great depths of China. [When *La Belle et la Bête* was presented at a gala in Shanghai, Mei Lan Fang, 'the King of Actors', famous particularly for his female roles, read this letter from Jean Cocteau].

L'Aigle à deux têtes

My intention, this time, was to transfer a play to the screen while keeping its theatrical character. It was in some senses a matter of walking, invisibly, around the stage and catching the different aspects and nuances in the play, the urgency and the facial expressions that escape a spectator who cannot follow them in detail from a seat in the stalls.

Apart from that, I had noticed how effective a play becomes when you have a bird's-eye view of it, for example from the flies, that is to say from the viewpoint of a voyeur. The audience is enclosed with the characters in a room lacking its fourth wall and listens to them on equal terms, without the element of mystery conferred on scenes of intimacy by the whimsical shape of a keyhole.

L'Aigle à deux têtes is not History. It is a story, an invented story lived out by imaginary heroes, and I should never have dared venture into the realistic world of cinema without being able to rely on the help of Christian Bérard. He has a genius for *situating* whatever he touches, for giving it a depth in time and space and an appearance of truth that are literally inimitable.

The film takes its inspiration from a more recent period than the stage play: this is the time when Sarah Bernhardt was young and when great ladies, princesses or actresses, discovered sport in long dresses and Chinese ornaments.

My queen is no longer a queen: the king has died, assassinated on the evening of their wedding day. But she still reigns, thanks to the power which she exerts over her people's imagination. She hides in her castles. She wears a veil. She does not show her face. In short, as the police minister says, 'she has an obtrusive invisibility'.

The king's mother, the archduchess, is afraid of this obtrusive invisibility. Her éminence grise, the Comte de Foëhn, chief of police, terrorizes small groups of anarchists and families living in clandestinity, who tarnish the queen's good name, accusing her of every sort of imagined vice.

They exploit the rebellious spirit of a sincere young anarchist who is chosen to kill the queen, but his rebellion is only a disguised form of love. His extraordinary resemblance to King Frédéric is what convinces the anarchists, and probably the police and the Comte de Foëhn.

The police intend to organize a fake manhunt and allow young Stanislas to rid the kingdom of someone who is standing in the archduchess' way: the archduchess is jealous of this power which is impossible to control. On the night of her arrival in Krantz (the castle where the king and queen went on the night of their wedding), the queen, who enjoys shocking the court, gives a provincial ball at which she is not going to appear. She tells the Duc de Willerstein, her aide-de-camp, and Mlle Berg, her reader, a young spy in the pay of the archduchess, to receive the guests in her place.

During the ball, she is to take supper in her room with the king's ghost, listening to the waltzes that he loved.

It is on this night of the ball at Krantz that Stanislas, pursued by the dogs and firearms of the police, falls into the queen's room after climbing away from them. He faints, the queen hides him, nurses him and explains, in answer to his obstinate silence, that she is treating him as an equal because she considers him her death, her angel of death. She wants to die, but will let fate decide. 'You are my fate,' she tells him, 'and this fate is pleasing to me.'

The killing needs to be done quickly. Stanislas was an assassin. He has missed his chance. He has to become a hero. That is more difficult.

The film shows the three days that the queen and her murderer spend together: she pretends to have requested that he come, by these fanciful means, to be her new reader.

There is no longer any protocol between them. The queen takes off her veil, walks about, speaks, insults and is insulted, tosses or bows her head. As we guess, she is on a precipitous descent towards love.

The Comte de Foëhn, warned of what is going on, offers to assist Stanislas in his political cause. Stanislas refuses. Foëhn has him arrested. He leaves him free until the queen sets out, after being persuaded by Stanislas to return to her capital and try to carry out a coup d'état.

Stanislas realizes that there is no escape from the dilemma of their love. Loving him, the queen has discarded in her room a phial of poison that she always kept with her, in a capsule which takes a quarter of an hour to dissolve.

Stanislas poisons himself with it and wants to see the queen once more. She discovers the empty phial and confronts Stanislas, deciding to act out an atrocious deception. She insults him and makes him believe that she has been ridiculing him, until he eventually stabs her.

Still standing, she walks and talks like Empress Elizabeth of Austria on the landing-stage at Geneva. She admits that she loves him. They die at almost the same moment, just as the queen was about to show herself, unveiled, to her escorts.

A drama of this kind would be unacceptable, and almost impossible to tell, unless it was interpreted by superb actors who could instill grandeur and life into it. Edwige Feuillère and Jean Marais, applauded evening after evening in their parts in the play, surpass themselves on the screen and give of themselves, as I suggested above, everything that they cannot give us on the stage.

George Auric's music and the Strauss waltzes at the Krantz ball make up the liquid in which this drama of love and death is immersed.

In *L'Aigle à deux têtes* — as a film (since I consider that this means of expression, this art form of cinematography, obliges us to address the masses without abandoning our prerogatives as artists) — I wanted (as far as possible, naturally) to stifle intellect under action and to make my characters act out their thoughts rather than express them in speech. I took this notion to the point of inventing an almost heraldic psychology for them, that is to say, one as far from ordinary psychology as the animals represented on heraldic shields are unlike animals as they really are: a smiling lion, for example, a unicorn kneeling before a virgin, or an eagle with a scroll in its beak.

This does not mean that the psychology is untrue, but that it is more real and more emphatic in the way it is expressed; nothing more.

One example, among many, might be the habit that a queen has of giving orders, and this habit inclining her to admit her love in a moment, when another person would have been less direct about it — with, added to this habit, a refinement of spirit that obliges the queen to overcome her natural inclination and disregard a delicacy that she despises in other people. This insolent daring is precisely what at first repels Stanislas, who considers it ridiculous, then gradually astonishes him and changes to admiration and love. This explains the workings of the soul in this film.

Otherwise, Bérard and I looked for inspiration, without allowing a single detail to tie us down, to the peculiar atmosphere of those royal houses in which what is called decadence when applied to poets (although it is only their particular way of behaving) emerges as a sort of madness, through a naïve struggle against conformity and custom.

It is this that incites the queen to give a ball on the anniversary of the king's death, to stay away from it and, from force of habit, to try to kill habit by creating a form of ceremonial for herself in her room, a ritual with the king's ghost.

Only one detail was historical: the final stabbing and the fact that a famous empress could walk around for a long time with a dagger under her shoulder blade. The rest — the places, characters and events — is the pure product of my imagination.

It is difficult for me to imagine cinematography as an industry, because it is not my profession. Cinematography is a means of expression for me, like any other. It is an art, a very great art and perhaps the only one belonging to the people. As far as I am concerned, it is the ink of light with which I am entitled to write whatever I like (I am not talking about the script). In *L'Aigle à deux têtes* , I wanted to make a theatrical film.

It has been said of *L'Aigle à deux têtes* that it is a triumph of bad taste. Of course: it could not have been better put. Christian Bérard and Wakhévitch wanted to depict the bad taste of royalty. We are in the period after the Goncourts. Mallarmé, Manet and the Impressionists have discovered the Japanese style, that also appealed to queens and great actresses. *L'Aigle*, apart from the ballroom which was copied from the Prince of Wales's pagoda in Bath, exhibits the bric-a-brac from the studios of Marie Bashkirtseff and Sarah Bernhardt.

I know the faults of the film, but unfortunately the expense of the medium and the constraints of time that it imposes on us, prevent us from correcting our faults. Cinematography costs too much.

In *L'Aigle*, I shot five hundred metres of film of Edwige Feullière speaking entirely alone. Without her, this achievement would have been impossible. It became possible because she moves with the talent of a Chinese actor and because the intensity of Jean Marais' silence perfectly matches her actions and the authority of her words.

At the end of the film, it is not Marais' backward fall (made possible by his daring) that I find sensational, but his face which decomposes progressively as he mounts the stairs.

The queen in *L'Aigle* is not seriously comparable to Empress Elizabeth of Austria. Bérard looked most of all to the model of Queen Victoria and Queen Alexandra. It is important to attribute the queen's boldness in declaring her love to the unintentional tactlessness and the habit of giving orders that are typical of a ruler, and interpreted as pride or immodesty. It is when Stanislas notices this mania for giving orders, after the Mameluk's entrance, that he realizes their love is an illusion.

I should certainly not have dared to write the final scene, without the famous example of Empress Elizabeth. Yet the stabbing in *L'Aigle* has nothing to do with the one on the landing-stage at Geneva. The only similarity involves a clinical phenomenon and strength of mind. Might I add the scene of the trapeze, in a long dress, described by Christomanos?

If one accepts that cinematography is an art, one is bound to set oneself a problem in every film and try to solve it. In *Les Parents terribles*, what I determined to do was the opposite of what I did in *L'Aigle*: to de-theatricalize a play, to film it in chronological order and to catch the characters by surprise from the indiscreet angle of the camera. In short, I wanted to watch a family through the keyhole instead of observing its life from a seat in the stalls.

Les Parents terribles

You ask what form my gratitude to my colleagues on this film would take. Here it is.

Mmes de Bray and Dorziat

In the tennis match between Madame de Bray and Madame Dorziat, in which almost every ball is sliced or placed on the line, you are amazed by their speed and may wonder who holds her racket best. One plays with her guts, the other with her head, and this makes them incomparable in roles which demand precisely that difference in style.

Josette Day

Josette Day immediately hits the right note and is not afraid of making herself ugly when her features are contorted by tears — and it is not easy for her to make herself ugly. She never falls into excess or commits one of those lapses in discretion which the audience, alas, confuses with depth of feeling and to which actors stoop too easily. She is the ideal interpreter of a very difficult character who is, for that reason, expelled from the circle of a stifling family.

Jean Marais

Jean Marais triumphed in the role of Michel on the first night, in 1939. But then he was the same age as the character: he plunged into it and swam by instinct. Now it is a matter of great art. He composes the part, invents it, controls it. As soon as he is in danger of heightening the emotional temperature by facile means, he compensates with some comic effect. His astonishing method of always playing contrary to the blandishments of the audience and the expectations of the critics is a noble lesson in theatre and cinematography. Without his intuition, it would have been impossible to film *Les Parents terribles*. The film would be implausible and Léo's remark: 'To have seen nothing, one must be blind as Michel and my sister are blind,' would fall flat.

Germaine Dermoz, Berthe Bovy, Serge Reggiani and (Daniel) Gélin were outstanding on the stage. But the play was written for Yvonne de Bray and Jean Marais. On the screen they rewrite it in concrete images with a wonderful understanding of the text. Moreover, they are alike and have the same rhythm in their work.

Marcel André

Marcel André demonstrates one of the mysteries of cinematography: a screenwriter does not tell a story. It is the screen that tells it. In a sense, the story tells itself. Marcel André's gestures contradict all the rules and he is right. It is no longer one of my characters speaking. He escapes analysis. He is Georges — a Georges born in the wings and in the camera.

Michel Kelber

Michel Kelber and Tiquet gave me the keyhole through which I indiscreetly observe the family with its slamming doors. But this keyhole is the one against which children press their eyes and deform the world to suit themselves.

Christian Bérard

Bérard put my five fish in their aquarium, an aquarium with very little water, and a submarine growth which is the admirable and atrocious furniture of our childhood. I think that only Christian Bérard, by an ingenious piece of design, could get Yvonne de Bray's old dressing-gown to follow her authoritarian gait which, like her voice, resembles no other.

Georges Auric

Auric emphasized the entrance of certain emotions for me, just as melodrama used to emphasize the entry of characters. This use of a single, very brief musical motif is completely new in the history of cinematography.

Mme Douarinou-Sadoul

Jacqueline Sadoul added the punctuation that I had forgotten to include because of the speed at which I wrote. She put in the circumflex accents, the acute accents and the grave accents.

The producers (Les Films Ariane)

Finally my producers, who were not producers, but friends who came daily to visit us in our caravan.

Yvonne de Bray on Screen

The secret of Mme Yvonne de Bray's greatness is a secret even from her. Everything is weakened once it is made explicit. Mme de Bray derives her greatness from the fact that she makes none of her talents explicit.

It is not knowing her own strength that gives Mme de Bray her astonishing patience. For years and years she does not act. She becomes a spectator. She does not try to prove her genius. She lives and expends in living the gifts that she expended on stage in the days of Henri Bataille.

Doubtless it is because she lives with no thought of imitating life that she can accumulate the treasure which she expends, suddenly, out of the blue, for our delight.

Even so, one must know how to wait. And Mme de Bray does. She can only become more beautiful, because she has that animal something that distinguishes her from other women as it distinguished Sarah Bernhardt, Réjane and Colette whose lion's eyes she also possesses.

While in *L' Aigle à deux têtes* I wanted to make a theatrical film, with speech, gestures and actions from the theatre, in *Les Parents terribles* I wanted to 'de-theatricalize' a play, to surprise it through a keyhole and vary the viewpoint to make a film.

Mme de Bray agreed to the experiment. She never appears to act. It was enough for me to leave her free, in front of the

most indiscreet of machines: the camera. I begged her to take
no notice of it. It was not her place to worry about us, but
ours to worry about her. What did it matter if she looked at
the camera or if her hand came into the foreground like a
swiftly passing bird? The main thing was to capture, in an
instant, her childlike gaze and her marvellous voice, huge,
grating, soft, hard, made of velvet and metal.

I might add that if I had had any anxieties, they would
have been groundless. In two days, Yvonne de Bray had
guessed what was needed and adapted to her own method
techniques that are considered the most difficult of all to
learn.

Nothing with Yvonne de Bray seems to come from the
head. Everything comes from the heart and the guts, and
everything is radiant.

And, more than that, she is modest. She asks you to tell
her how a line should be said, which is amusing. And you
can do it. She immediately adapts the intonation to the
measure of her soul.

While we were making *L'Aigle*, it amused her to play an
old judge's wife, a five-minute bit part which involved
announcing the news that the queen would not take part in
the ball.

A journalist mentions her in the role of the archduchess.
This was a mistake as far as the film is concerned, but quite
right in the case of Mme de Bray whom one cannot ever
imagine appearing in a supporting role.

I hope that the audience realizes precisely what Mme de
Bray has contributed to cinematography in her role as the
mother in *Les Parents terribles*. It is incalculable. [*L'Ecran
français*, N° 176, November 9, 1948].

Orphée

I wanted to deal with the problem of what is decreed in advance and what is not decreed in advance — in short, with free will.

When I make a film, it is a sleep in which I am dreaming. Only the people and places of the dream matter. I have difficulty making contact with others, as one does when half-asleep. If a person is asleep and someone else comes into the sleeper's room, this other person does not exist. He or she exists only if introduced into the events of the dream. Sunday is not a real day of rest for me, I try to go back to sleep as quickly as possible.

Death in my film is not Death represented symbolically by an elegant young woman, but the Death of Orphée. Each of us has our own which takes charge of us from the moment of birth. So Orphée's Death, exceeding her authority, becomes Cégeste's, and Cégeste says to her — when she asks: 'Do you know who I am?' — 'You are my Death', and not: 'You are Death'.

Realism in unreality is a constant pitfall. People can always tell me that this is possible, or that is impossible; but do we understand anything about the workings of fate? This is the mysterious mechanism that I have tried to make tangible. Why is Orphée's Death dressed in this way, or that? Why does she travel in a Rolls, and why does Heurtebise appear and disappear at will in some circumstances, but submit to human laws in others? This is the eternal why that obsesses thinkers, from Pascal to the least of poets.

Any unexpected phenomenon in nature disturbs us and confronts us with puzzles that we are sometimes unable to solve. No one has yet fathomed the true secret of an ants' nest or a beehive. The mimicry and spots of animals surely prove that some species have thought for a long time about becoming invisible; but we know nothing more than that.

I wanted to touch lightly on the most serious problems, without idle theorizing. So the film is a thriller which draws on myth from one side and the supernatural from the other.

I have always liked the no man's land of twilight where mysteries thrive. I have thought, too, that cinematography is superbly adapted to it, provided it takes the least possible advantage of what people call the supernatural. The closer you get to a mystery, the more important it is to be realistic. Radios in cars, coded messages, shortwave signals and power cuts are all familiar to everybody and allow me to keep my feet on the ground.

Nobody can believe in a famous poet whose name has been invented by a writer. I had to find a mythical bard, the bard of bards, the Bard of Thrace. And his story is so enchanting that it would be crazy to look for another. It provides the background on which I embroider. I do nothing more than to follow the cadence of all fables which are modified in the long run according to who tells the story. Racine and Molière did better. They copied antiquity. I always advise people to copy a model. It is by the impossibility of doing the same thing twice and by the new blood that is infused into the old frame that the poet is judged.

Orphée's Death and Heurtebise reproach Orphée for asking questions. Wanting to understand is a peculiar obsession of mankind.

There is nothing more vulgar than works that set out to prove something. *Orphée*, naturally, avoids even the appearance of trying to prove anything.

'What were you trying to say?' This is a fashionable question. I was trying to say what I said.

All arts can and must wait. They may even wait to live until after the artist is dead. Only the ridiculous costs of cinematography force it to instant success, so it is satisfied with being mere entertainment.

With *Orphée*, I decided to take the risk of making a film as if cinematography could permit itself the luxury of waiting — as if it was the art which it ought to be.

Beauty hates ideas. It is sufficient to itself. A work is beautiful as a person is beautiful. The beauty I mean (the beauty of Piero della Francesca, Uccello and Vermeer), causes an erection of the soul. An erection is unarguable. Few people are capable of having one: most, as in the famous drawing by Forain, consider that 'it is much better to talk.'

Our age is becoming dried out with ideas. It is the child of the Encyclopaedists. But having an idea is not enough: the idea must have us, haunt us, obsess us, become unbearable to us.

Le Sang d'un poète was based on the poet's need to go through a series of deaths and to be reborn in a shape closer to his real being. There, the theme was played with one finger, and inevitably so, because I had to invent a craft that I did not know. In *Orphée*, I have orchestrated the theme, and this is why the two films are related, twenty years apart.

My film could not stand the slightest degree of fantasy, which would have seemed to me like breaking my own rules, so, as I was inventing the rules, I had to make them comply with numbers that were governed by nothing outside their relationships to one another.

If I made Heurtebise disappear, once by using the mirror and once on the spot, this was because I thought it important to preserve the degree of latitude that intrigues entomologists, although its laws escape them.

I have often been asked about the figure of the glassvendor: he was the only one able to illustrate the saying that there is nothing so hard to break as the habit of one's job; since, although he died very young, he still persists in crying his wares in a region where windowpanes are meaningless.

Once the machinery had been set in motion, everyone had to go with it, so that in the scene when he returns to the house, Marais succeeded in being comical without going beyond the limits of taste and with no break between lyricism and operetta.

The same is true of François Périer whose mockery never becomes unkind or makes him seem to be taking advantage of his supernatural powers. Nothing was more demanding than the role of Orphée, grappling with the injustices of the youth of literature. He does not seem to me to have secrets

which he divines and which deceive him. He proves his
greatness only through that of the actor. Here again, Marais
illuminates the film for me with his soul.

Among the misconceptions which have been written about
Orphée, I still see Heurtebise described as an angel and the
Princess as Death.

In the film, there is no Death and no angel. There can be
none. Heurtebise is a young Death serving in one of the
numerous sub-orders of Death, and the Princess is no more
Death than an air hostess is an angel.

I never touch on dogmas. The region that I depict is a
border on life, a no man's land where one hovers between life
and death. The tribunal bears the same relationship to the
supreme tribunal as the investigating magistrate to the trial.
The Princess says: 'Here, you go from one tribunal to the
next.'

Critics describe as *longueurs*, the waves between the knots,
the passages of relaxation between moments of intense
activity.

Shakespeare is all longs and shorts: this is what makes him
worthy of attention. The English do not notice the *longueurs*
in Shakespeare because they know they are coming and
respect them.

When Marais is praised for his acting in *Orphée*, he replies:
'The film plays my parts for me.'

The three basic themes of *Orphée* are:

1. The successive deaths through which a poet must pass
before he becomes, in that admirable line from Mallarmé, *tel
qu'en lui-même enfin l'éternité le change* — changed into himself
at last by eternity.

2. The theme of immortality: the person who represents
Orphée's Death sacrifices herself and abolishes herself to
make the poet immortal.

3. Mirrors: we watch ourselves grow old in mirrors. They
bring us closer to death.

The other themes are a mixture of Orphic and modern
myth: for example, cars that talk (the radio receivers in
cars).

I should point out that the scene of the return to the house is comic. To paraphrase, when a Frenchman has fallen out of love with a woman, and can't stand the sight of her, what he says, literally, is: 'I can't see her any more'. [*Cinémonde*, N° 842, September 25, 1950].

A poet's film is like a huge print run of one of his books. It is quite natural for many people not to accept this book, but its huge circulation multiplies our chances of touching some minds, the few people that, at one time, a poet would only reach in the long term, or after his death. Moreover, the experience of *Orphée* shows that these few people are count-less. Just as ten francs become a thousand, it seems that some rate of exchange is operating with the audience. People who like the film and write to me (I count them among the *countless few*) all complain about the rest of the audience in the Parisian cinema, which they consider a lifeless mass. They forget that without the cinema they could not have seen the film.

Orphée is a realistic film; or, to be more precise, observing Goethe's distinction between reality and truth, a film in which I express a truth peculiar to myself. If that truth is not the spectator's, and if his personality conflicts with mine and rejects it, he accuses me of lying. I am even astonished that so many people can still be penetrated by another's ideas, in a country noted for its individualism.

While *Orphée* does encounter some lifeless audiences, it also encounters others that are open to my dream and agree to be put to sleep and to dream it with me (accepting the logic by which dreams operate, which is implacable, although it is not governed by our logic).

I am only talking about the mechanics, since *Orphée* is not at all a dream in itself: through a wealth of detail similar to that which we find in dreams, it summarizes my way of living and my conception of life.

These receptive audiences are more and more so, the further north the film travels, or when a mass audience immerses itself in it sincerely, without the coldness of soul of

an élite or its fear of dipping its toes in dangerous waters that
might disturb what it is used to.

Already, when the wish to make such a film is transformed
into a concrete undertaking, everything is disturbed through
the machinery, actors, sets and unforeseeable events.

So I have to admit that the phenomenon of refraction
begins even before the work leaves me, and I run the
ultimate risk of the phenomenon of multiple refraction.

Marcenac's piece for *Ce soir* (since you have asked what I
think of it), provides me with a remarkable example of this
phenomenon of refraction, after a work has been launched.

And, just as the analysis of a film by a psychoanalyst can
tell us about some implications and some sources of a labour
that is all the less tightly under our control since the material
problems we encounter during it make us insensible to
tiredness and leave our unconscious quite free, so the
interpretation of one of our works by the mind of an outsider
can show it to us from a new, and revealing perspective.

How disturbed we should be, were there some machine
that would allow us to follow the strange progress of a story
as it winds its way through the thousand brains in a cinema!
No doubt, we should stop writing. We should be wrong to do
so, but it would be a hard lesson. What Jules de Noailles said
(recounted by Liszt), is true: 'You will see one day that it is
hard to speak about anything with anyone.' Yet it is equally
true that each person takes in or rejects the sustenance that
we offer, and that the people who absorb it, do so in their
own way; and this it is that determines the progress of a work
through the centuries, because if a work were to send back
only a perfect echo, the result would be a kind of pleonasm,
an inert exchange, a dead perfection.

Obviously I was quite stupefied when, one Sunday in the
country, I heard *Orphée* on the radio and caught the following
remark, intended to depict the no man's land between life
and death: 'They go through the subterranean cathedrals of
hell'. But when a serious and attentive man (whom I do not
know personally) takes the trouble to recall a plot and, in
several stages, with an almost childlike elegance, tries to

draw a simple and easy-to-read storyline out of this very complex plot, without abandoning either his personal view-point, or precision, I can only refrain from criticizing him. To do so would be as inappropriate as those critics who hastily condemn a work that is the product of thirty years of research. [*Les Lettres françaises*, November 16, 1950].

Le Testament d'Orphée

Any young aviator nowadays can perform the acrobatic feats that I once performed with Garros — at a time when only Garros and Pégoud were capable of them. Any young pianist can cope with the virtuoso passages that were once within the range of only Liszt and Chopin. The same is true of technical progress in cinematography. When I made *Le Sang d'un poète*, thirty years ago, I knew nothing about the craft and no one in the world could have taught me what I did not know. I had to invent a technique for my own use and tackle a thousand problems to discover what was later to become a childishly simple matter. Too much progress smoothes the way and makes the mind lazy. Nowadays, any young film-maker is able to produce a good film, just as any young painter knows better than just to daub the paint on the canvas. In his speech on being received into the French Academy, Voltaire already warned of the danger of technical progress. 'A people that is too skilled,' he said, 'and too intelligent, ceases to press forward'. By this he means that the exceptional and the outstanding vanish and are replaced by a fair average.

This is why I gave up using film, even though it provides us with a genuine vehicle for poetry, in the sense that it permits one to show unreality with a realism that forces the spectator to believe in it.

Bit by bit, when I learned that *Le Sang d'un poète*, a film made for a few intimate friends, had been showing for thirty years in all the capital cities in the world, and most remarkably in New York, where it has stayed for the past seventeen years in the same cinema, establishing a record for the longest-ever 'exclusive' run, I thought that it would be interesting to come full circle and end my career in films with a piece similiar to *Le Sang d'un poète*, which would force me to overcome different obstacles from the earlier ones.

A free film, without any commercial conditions attached, intended for the vast audience of young people educated in cinematheques throughout the world, which is never offered the kind of films that it thirsts for.

Moreover, I think that one of the main faults in cinematography comes from the fact that people never consider a variety of ways of launching a film, and force young people to do old people's work and take on old habits, or otherwise their films will stay in a trunk and never manage to get out.

Maybe it was necessary for an old man — that is, one who is freer than the young to be young — to open a sealed door and take the head of a procession that is only waiting to start its march.

When I said on television and the radio that my film, *Le Testament d'Orphée*, 'would have neither head nor tail, but a soul', I was making a serious jest. In fact, I am astonished — at a time when painters have sacrificed the subject to the art of painting and abolished the model or the pretext for their work — that cineasts, harassed by producers who think that they know the audience and have never outgrown the childish desire to be told a story, demand a 'subject' and an *excuse*, when the manner of saying and showing things, and furnishing the screen, are a thousand times more important than the story you tell.

Unfortunately, the audience (and, for films, it is vast) is still at the same level as the lady who, having an aversion to colonial soldiers, announced that she could never like Van Gogh's *Zouave*; or the gentleman who was allergic to roses and could not hang a bunch of roses by Fantin-Latour or Renoir on his wall.

But the time has come to destroy these ridiculous taboos and to educate the cinema audience, just as the public has been educated for art exhibitions. Otherwise the young, in the field of cinematography, will never be young, but condemned always to submit to the bad habits of producers, distributors and cinema managers.

It is ridiculous to say that the cinema has nothing to do with what is rare. This is to deny it its role as a Muse, and the Muses should be shown in an attitude of expectation. They are waiting for beauty, which at first is disconcerting and appears ugly, to make its slow inroads into people's minds. Unfortunately, the ridiculous costs of cinema force it to bow before the idol of instant success.

This hideous idol of our age — this detestable dogma — must be overcome. We shall not succeed overnight. But I shall be proud if my efforts contribute in some way and if, at some future time, young people are indebted to me for a little of their power to bring out a film as a poet publishes a book of poems, without being subject to the American imperatives of the best-seller.

'The Golden Calf is always made of clay': I acknowledge authorship of this sort of play on words, without shame and without any fear of reproach. It falls under the same heading as a pronouncement by the Delphic Oracle. For the time will come when the ideological money of cinema and the abstract fortunes that it displays, will no longer stand in the way of the reasonable sums that the slightest film requires, which are immediately recovered if the film has something new to offer and does not simply dole out what those who despise the people imagine they crave. It is those so-called 'élites' that are blocking our way: the people are sensitive to beauty, even if it disturbs them. And our films, condemned on the grounds that they are made by a minority, should break through the barrier and fall into the majority which judges more and more by instinct and has not yet been made immune to novelty by the routine of fashion.

My hostility to Descartes is so intense that I might sometimes be the Descartes of Anti-Cartesianism.

The more I respect Pascal's half-open circle, which chance can penetrate by surprise, the more I hate the closed circle of a philosopher who has been contradicted by the progress of knowledge and who symbolizes the French people's frightful mania for understanding everything. Why? This is the leitmotiv of France: 'Explain what you were trying to paint.' We are only a step away from having to explain what music means: as in the Pastoral Symphony, where the auditorium is delighted when it can recognize the cuckoo and the peasant dances.

In fact, everything that can be explained or demonstrated is vulgar. It really is time that mankind admitted that it is living on an incomprehensible planet, where people walk heads downwards in relation to the natives of the Antipodes, and that infinity, eternity, space-time and other fantasies will always be incomprehensible to our minute understanding, reduced to its three dimensions — even if the poor earthling manages, with great difficulty, to break away from the Earth (to which he remains attached by an umbilical cord) and to visit the Moon, which is an ancient, dead earth, not much further away from us than Asnières or Bois-Colombes.

The Moon was an earth, the Earth will be a moon. The Sun will be an earth, and so on. This is all that we know of a horrifying mechanical process in which we have given ourselves the leading role and in which we are nothing — a few microbes attached to a patch of mould that, because we are so small, we can see as pleasant landscapes and charming countryside.

Le Testament d'Orphée: the title has no direct connection with my film. It meant that I was bequeathing this last visual poem to all the young people who have believed in me, despite the total incomprehension with which I am surrounded on the part of my contemporaries.

I would emphasize that this film is the contrary of an intellectual, or 'art' film.

I should like to be able to say: 'I don't think, therefore I am.' All thought paralyzes action. And a film is a succession of acts. Thought weighs it down and embellishes it in an unbearable and pretentious manner. Poetry is the opposite of 'poetic'. As soon as someone aspires to being a poet, that person ceases to be one and the poetry makes its escape. This is when people recognize its rear view, and congratulate themselves for being subtle enough to understand it.

In *Le Testament d'Orphée*, events follow one another as they do in sleep, when our habits no longer control the forces within us or the logic of the unconscious, foreign to reason. A dream is strictly mad, strictly absurd, strictly magnificent and strictly atrocious. But no part of us ever judges it. We submit to it, without activating the abominable human tribunal that accords itself the right to condemn or absolve.

Otherwise, it is probable that the plot of my film is made up of signs and meanings. However, I know nothing of this and can only accept it in the shape of a machine for manufacturing meanings. I should add that the signs and meanings that the audience will discover in it must doubtless have a basis in which the deeper self that transcends my superficial self comes to the fore.

Let me repeat what I have often said: *I am a cabinet-maker, not a medium.* My task is limited to making a fine table — if others put their hands on it and force it to speak, this does not concern me, although it intrigues me in just the same way as it does those who call up the spirits of the dead, since our works, the second after they have been written, become posthumous ones.

I am 69 and I shall be 70 on July 5, 1959. I act in almost every scene in the film, with the help of my adopted son, the painter Edouard Dermit, who has already done me the service of playing Paul in *Les Enfants terribles* and Cégeste in *Orphée*.

I think that when I was young (at the time of *Le Sang d'un poète*), it was better to give my role (ideologically) to Rivero. At that time I might have been found attractive. Now that I am old, it takes courage to appear in my own role as the poet, with none of the advantages of physical appeal. As for Edouard Dermit, having formerly abandoned him in the famous region which is neither life nor death in the film *Orphée*, I make him reappear in *Le Testament d'Orphée* purely so that he can lead me from one blunder to the next until I am obliged to disappear with him and leave a world where, as he says, 'you know quite well you have no place.'

At the end of the *Testament* — and I have just this minute realized that this is related to the scene with the commissioner in my play *Orphée* — I accompany two police motorcyclists, vaguely similiar to the celebrated motorcyclists of the Princess; and after my disappearance and that of my son, a jazzy car sweeps away my identity papers which the motorcyclist has dropped and which, on contact with the soil, have become the irrational flower that I try to revive so that I can offer it to Minerva, goddess of Reason.

In any case, Minerva refuses to accept it, as something dead, and pierces me with her lance. Then, as in all my myths, my death is a fake. It is *one of my deaths*, and the gypsies sob over my empty tombstone.

I walk away and pass the Sphinx, and Oedipus led by Antigone. I do not even notice them. Like Prince André in *War and Peace*, who dreamed of meeting Napoleon and does not even glance at him because, lying wounded on the battlefield, he is gazing at the splendour of the clouds. This is the point at which the meeting with the motorcyclists and the abduction by Cégeste occur.

You will guess that all these scenes represent nothing symbolic. They came into my mind in that vague sleepwalking state without which I would never dare to write.

Poets are only the humble servants of a self which is more ourselves than we are: it hides in the depth of our being and dictates its orders.

We are endlessly compromised by this self, so that it can avoid a beating, just as Don Giovanni disguises Leporello in his clothes, so that he will be beaten in his place.

People have said a lot about famous actors, like Yul Brynner and Jean Marais (among others), who reportedly appear in my work even though their names are not on the credits. This is true, in the sense that, for friendship's sake, it amused them to take small parts in a film that in no way resembles any of theirs.

In the same way, well-known people appeared in *Le Sang d'un poète*.

I find it hard to say any more. It is not that I am cultivating secrecy, which I find pretentious and ridiculous, but because I think that a cinematographic work can no more be described than a painting.

Its 'matter' and 'manner' are what counts, not the things represented in it.

In any case, I do not expect any of the success with this film that rewards the splendours of cinematography. A few friends and personalities in cinema circles have agreed to make possible an undertaking that, I repeat, responds to none of the demands of cinematography. It is *something else*, that 'something' which mysteriously attaches itself to certain stars in sport or the music hall. And when people protest that the sportsmen I admire are not sportsmen or that the pictures I like are not pictures, and I ask them: 'Well then, what are they?', these people answer: 'I don't know — *something else*.' Well, I think that, when it comes down to it, that 'something else' is the best definition of poetry.

This time, in my film, I was careful to make the special effects serve the internal, not the external development of the film. They should help me to make this line of development as supple as the thought processes of '*un homme qui gamberge*' — to use a splendid term not found in our dictionary.

'*Gamberger*' means to let the mind follow its own, uncontrolled course; and, while it is different from dreaming, daydreaming or reverie, allowing our most intimate notions (those most tightly imprisoned within us) to escape and flee unseen past the guards. Everything else is just 'thesis' or 'flair': I am repelled by both.

A thesis forces us to 'buckle the wheel', to twist it so that it will obediently follow an artificial line, while flair incites us for no valid reason to accelerate, slow down or reverse, and although it is very tempting to use these devices, the effect of surprise only carries weight when they are integrated into the task and remain unobtrusive.

If the frivolous and thoughtless people who judge our films

knew the discipline involved in montage, they would regard
us with some trepidation and denounce us to the ecclesiastic
court as alchemists.

It is true that we manufacture gold. But this gold has no
currency except for a few rare and attentive souls. I once
happened to mention the wonderful film *Lady Lou* (Mae
West) to a man of the world who was far superior to most of
his kind and fanatical about a film that he had seen five
times. When I reminded him of certain episodes (including
the one where Mae West hides the dead woman by pretend-
ing to comb her hair), he admitted that he could not
remember them and was astonished that I could. In short,
he had seen nothing, merely felt a vague sense of enjoyment
of the whole, without being struck by any of those details that
cost us so much effort to create.

And, I repeat, this man of the world was far more
intelligent than those of his class.

But if all these details had not existed, the whole of the film
would not have impressed him or left any trace in his
memory.

Undeniably, most spectators of my film will say that it is a
folly and incomprehensible. They will not be entirely wrong,
since there are times when I do not understand it myself and
when I am on the point of admitting defeat and making my
excuses to those who believed in me. But experience has
taught me that one must on no account give up things that
had a meaning when they appear to lose it, so I make the
effort to overcome my weakness and force myself to feel the
same confidence in myself that I feel with regard to others
when I admire and respect them. In short, I put confidence
in that *other*, that stranger whom we become a few minutes
after creating some work.

Does life 'mean something'? I wonder; and art often
consists in trying to construct an artificial meaning for it and
deprive it of that mysterious charm, of 'God's portion' as
Gide calls it, and which, in his work, might frequently be
called 'the devil's portion'.

The first question that journalists ask me is the familiar

one in France: 'What is the story?' If I reply candidly: 'there is none', they look at me with the dread that people feel when confronted by a madman. But it is true. *There is none.* I exploit the realism of settings, people, gestures, words and music to obtain a mould for abstraction of thought — or, I might put it, to construct a castle, without which it is difficult to imagine a ghost. If the castle was itself ghostly, the ghost would lose its power to appear and terrify.

So, I insist, an abstract film is not a film similar to so-called abstract painting, content to imitate naïvely a painter's blobs of colour and balancing effects. An abstract film should not give form to *a thought* but to *thought* itself, that unknown force which rules by no other virtue than that of being a force more forceful than the rest and faster than speed — force and speed in itself.

This is the force that I try to obey and not to hold back with that much-admired intelligence which transcends nothing except stupidity.

My two major bugbears are *the poetic* and *the intellectual*. Unfortunately, they rule the world and drive out the winged world that the poet occasionally succeeds in ensnaring. When I was young I used to sign my drawings and writings 'Jean l'Oiseleur' — Jean the Bird-Catcher.

It was Jean l'Oiseleur who made *Le Testament d'Orphée* in the hope of touching a few fraternal souls in this sad world. Goethe said: 'It is when we hug ourselves that we may encounter our soul-brothers.' This is a dangerous slogan in an age when people are governed by depersonalization, which tries to abolish the differences and contrasts which used to give the universe a human face and succeeded in crushing monotony and automatism.

Here is my wish and my oracle: 'In the long term, depersonalization will fill people's souls with such gloom that there will be a new victory of the singular over the plural, that the majority will cease to consider itself the supreme authority, that the sheep will no longer take the place of the shepherd and that minorities, abandoning their dream of becoming the majority, will once more become like

the priests who guarded the secrets of the temple; in short,
the creative spirit, the highest form of the spirit of contradic-
tion, will obliterate the modern "do-as-you-wish" — the
false freedom of action that is taught to American children,
which deprives children, young people, heroes and artists of
their essential motivation: *disobedience*.' [This text is given
here for the first time in its complete form. Extensive extracts
appeared in *Le Monde*, July 25, 1959; *La Table Ronde*, N° 149,
May 1960; and *La Saison cinématographique 1960*, among
others].

My dear Louis,
Twenty years of quarrels and reconciliations, escapes and
returns, have woven the cloth of our friendship so tightly that
not even an Iago could unpick it. This fine material is
composed of numberless gold threads crossing, plaited
together and contradicting one another. For there are pro-
found similiarities and profound differences between us; in
short, the contrasts, the struggles of light and shade, the
conflicting perspectives and the noble faults (the truth that
Goethe contrasts with reality), without which a work of art
would be a mere pleonasm and the relationship between
friends a form of friendly flirtation.

This is why I am answering your request for an article
with a letter; but don't worry: it will be shorter than the
endless pages in which, while I was reading it, I expressed
my love for your wonderful novel *La Semaine sainte*.

You wanted an article on my film *Le Testament d'Orphée*.
Well, it is better that I should talk about it to you, as we
sometimes do in the rue de La Sourdière, in one of those
monologues for two voices when we accomplish the feat of
speaking and listening at one and the same time. Elsa[1] looks
up: 'You do not let anyone open their mouth!' And we laugh,
and carry on, taking revenge on that other obscure chatter-
box who dictates our works to us and leaves us very little

---

1 Aragon's wife, Elsa Triolet.

freedom for give-and-take. This leads me to tell you about the problems I have with the young muse of cinema who cannot agree to wait like her sisters, but condemns to immediacy poets who have become accustomed to wait in the wings and live for posterity.

The film should have been made in 1958. The delay came from the fact that the producers, eager to work with me, took fright when they read my screenplay and dialogues (after telling me that they did not even want to read them). One of them, to excuse himself for going back on his word, told a journalist: 'I cannot produce a film in which nothing happens.' The fact is that, in my opinion, nothing happens in any of this producer's films. But there are more people who accept *that* Nothing than people who can understand the richness of ours. The contours of a moving image can only describe themselves.

Art begins the moment that the artist departs from nature. And it is just when painters are departing from it to the point of abandoning pretexts, motives and models that, under pressure from the uncultured, cinematography is forcing young film-makers to choose 'a subject', like the painters of the Salon des Artistes Français in 1900 or competitors for the Prix de Rome.

Apart from that, the young have helped us so much, you and me, that I think the time has come for me to offer them some help in return by giving them a free work that meets their expectations, constantly disappointed by mere routine.

The cost of a film, and the desire to recoup these costs quickly, suggests a strange paradox: to carry conviction, youth must submit to old ways and avant-garde fashions, and only old age, thanks to the authority it has acquired, allows us to become free and to invent young works. The exhibition of Picasso's *Meniñas* provides further proof of this.

In short, the perspective gained by a delay which is unsuited to the style of cinematography caused a loss of momentum, opened my eyes on the darkness which conceals the best in ourselves, and revealed in me that transcendental idiocy called intelligence which transforms us from defend-

ents in the dock to judges on the bench and inflicts on us the
fatal constraints of criticism.

So here I am, becoming an audience, bemused by my
former spontaneity and, like Kipling's Kim in India when he
sees miracles and subterfuge superimposed, tempted to alter
my text, while knowing that this would be a ridiculous crime
against the spirit.

At present I am only studying to overcome in myself the
devil which, everyone knows, rules by panache and ruins the
instinctive forces of the heart and the soul.

I do accuse myself of the stupidity of having believed in
the privileges of age, while in fact I shall remain until I die
(and doubtless beyond that) a solitary sniper.

I was born that, and that I shall remain: the accused,
standing before his complacent judges.

We are often accused, my dear Louis, of talking about
ourselves. So who can restore things to their proper place in
an age when a humble workman like myself is treated as a
light-headed dabbler — a man who never accepts the
slightest task unless he is sure of being able to complete it?
And, since my changes of direction seem to throw off the
pack, it is surely normal that I should address myself to
someone whose magnificent agility causes us endless sur-
prise. ['Open Letter to Louis Aragon', *Les Lettres françaises*,
N° 785, August 6, 1959].

The danger for a film is that people become accustomed to
see it without giving it the attention that they would to a play
or a book. Despite this, it is a vehicle for ideas and poetry of
the first order, able to take the spectator into regions where
he had previously been led only by sleep and dreams. I often
think that it would be splendidly economical if a fakir were to
hypnotize a whole audience. He would show them a wonder-
ful spectacle and, in addition, order them not to forget it
when they woke up. And this is to some extent the role of the
screen: to exert a sort of hypnotic effect on the audience and
allow a large number of people to dream the same dream
together. The effect is hard to obtain in this country, where

every member of a crowd is an individualist who instinctively resists what is offered and considers the desire to persuade as an assault on the personality.

This time I did not set myself any problems to solve. I made the film in a reverie, with no regulation of any kind, as an experiment in bringing the darkness within me into the light.

With hindsight, I can see that the film is not properly speaking a film, but something that offered me the only means of expressing things that I carry within me — without properly understanding them — objectively and even directly: things which, as you may imagine, any other vehicle of thought like writing would force me to bring under the regulatory control of the intellect, while film licences one to live the work instead of describing it and, in addition, to make the invisible visible.

In *Le Testament d'Orphée*, I achieved such a perfect blend of truth and fable, realism and the unreal, that I am confused by it: it would be impossible for me to unravel the knot and attempt to analyze it.

The subtitle, 'Do Not Ask Me Why', means that I would be incapable of saying why I pursued a venture from beginning to end that responds to none of the constraints of cinematography.

The only obvious thing is that film, because of its potential for going backwards in time and overcoming its narrow limits, was the only suitable language in which to expose the obscurity within me and set it out on a table in the full light of day. Moreover, this feeling did not only apply to me. Maria Casarès, for example, had the impression that she was bringing the words and gestures of her role out of herself, and when François Périer had to make a rather unpleasant remark to me, he apologized, forgetting that I had written the line, as though he were ashamed of his responsibility for it. His delicacy and consideration when he talks to the professor comes from the fact that he is very fond of Crémieux, and was talking to Crémieux rather than to the scientist that Crémieux plays.

Throughout the film there was this duality, this blend that I might compare in the non-material world to the sensation, when you are rolling a marble with the end of the index and middle fingers crossed over, that creates the illusion of touching not one, but two marbles together.

Like me, Edouard Dermit plays himself, and at the same time the role of Cégeste which he took in the film *Orphée*; Maria Casarès and Périer, who also return to their roles from *Orphée*, do so not knowing, or pretending not to know, who Cégeste is. Perhaps they visit me because of the mysterious links that attach the creatures of his imagination to an author. I know that I am demanding a great effort from the audience and that it would be ridiculous to expect the spectators to take the trouble to unpick a tangle that I cannot unpick myself.

But it is possible to be carried away by an enigmatic atmosphere, including that of dreams, and I think that a work can intrigue without being understood and appeal without having to be proved mathematically or authenticated by the golden section.

PS 'Do you like beef stew?' 'Yes.' 'Do you understand it?' 'I have never considered the matter.' 'That sums it up.'

The more unreal a film is, the more realism it requires to convince the audience. Properly speaking, realism is assisted by habit which plugs the gaps and corrects mistakes.

If, on the other hand, a film is deliberately made up of mistakes, it is essential to sanctify them, that is to say to make them so undeniable that they become exemplary — *to make such gross errors that they cease to be errors.*

This is something that Picasso taught me: increasingly, he sets about sanctifying errors and making them stand out, to the point where the work escapes from being a bad copy of nature and exhibits the features of a superior race and reign, governed by men.

This was the rule I followed in *Le Testament d'Orphée*; and even when hindsight interposed the regulatory control of intelligence (the poet's worst enemy), I disregarded it. [*Arts*, N° 761, February 10, 1960]

My dear Régis Bastide,
What seems to me to give this film a new style is that after thirty years of research I have managed to arrange actions as one arranges words in constructing a poem.

This is in some respects an alchemical experiment, the transmutation of word into action.

It has happened that poetic words have been imposed on a plot. Here the words are unimportant and only the act counts. The scenes fit together, acquiring the significance of signs rather than any meaning, in the proper sense. I have no story to tell. I let events follow whatever path they wish. But instead of losing all control, as one does in dreams, I celebrate that marriage of the conscious with the unconscious which brings to birth the awesome and delightful monster called *poetry*.

The great mistake that has been made throughout the centuries is to confuse this monster with a petty imitator, its shadow puppet: with *the poetic*, which is as far from poetry as Molière's *précieuses ridicules* from Madame de La Fayette.

For this film in which I try to petrify thought, I chose places that are like veritable petrifying springs, mysterious streams that, I repeat, can achieve the metamorphosis of a script into acts. For example, the Val d'Enfer at Les Baux-de-Provence, so called because Dante lived there and was inspired by it in *The Divine Comedy*; or the Studio de la Victorine, in which a few accessories were enough to create a significant place surrounded by emptiness, on the model of the Chinese theatre, or else like our bedroom which we imagine to be outside the room when we doze and shut our eyes.

It has amused people to talk about stars agreeing to take bit parts in my film. This is a mistake. Unreality has even stricter laws than realism, because realism is assisted by habit while the unreal, because of its unexpected nature, requires extreme precision down to the last detail. There are very few characters in *Le Testament d'Orphée* and nothing is less easy to play than a small part since only a great talent can rapidly hit on the striking detail that a lesser talent will not discover except with time. My famous friends who answered my request accepted parts that a lot of unknown actors would have refused to play. But there will be no credits: recognize them if you will and if they act here, it is not because they are famous actors, but because they are my friends. They know that I am employing them on the same basis as the effects men, the electricians, the boom operator, the cameraman, or the admirable and adorable Claude Pinoteau, my right hand; in short, on the same basis as the whole of a team in which the least subordinate has that craftsman's genius without which a film would remain a mere procession of images.

Moreover, my film was not wealthy enough to afford so many actors, so I had to appeal to friends who would agree to make it for nothing. It so happened that these friends were famous actors. This is the real secret of the matter: it was my good fortune to be poor.

I hate the picturesque, the poetical, fantasy and symbols — all those old lifelines that the audience clings to whenever it falls out of its everyday comfort into the ocean of things that disturb it, which it avoids for fear of drowning.

Only a shipwreck is beautiful, only disobedience towards dead rules, only the accidental and the erroneous, provided man is strong enough to sanctify them and make them exemplary. An error ceases to be one if the person who commits it changes it into what Baudelaire called 'the most recent expression of Beauty'.

The problem for a work of art is that this recent expression of Beauty upsets habits, changes the rules of the game and at first sight resembles ugliness or a sort of Medusa's head. Things are still more difficult in cinematography, because the young Muse of Cinema, unlike her nine sisters, refuses to wait for new beauty to penetrate people's souls and eventually succeed in convincing them. She demands that one join her in the worship of immediacy, haste and hitching a ride, which is the crime committed by our impatient and turbulent age against the spirit. She is a spendthrift who wants a quick return for her money. She does not know that youth will not endure and imagines that there is a permanent race of the young, as there is of the old. It will be a long time yet before she understands her sacred mission, to become that tenth muse which, like the others and like the praying mantis, devours those whom she loves so that their work can live in their stead.

I am not a cineast. I am a poet who uses the camera as a suitable vehicle for allowing us all to dream the same dream together, a dream which is not a sleeping dream but one dreamed on one's feet, which is nothing other than unreal realism, something that is truer than the truth and which, one day, will be recognized as the distinguishing mark of our age.

My dear Régis,
Please forgive these words which are a little too serious to entertain a reader. But I have always considered poetry a priestly vocation and a sort of lay cloister, the Rule of which you agree to follow once and for all. I know full well that the public likes stories and stars and that it forces us to get up on the rostrum under the spotlights with the Miss Europes and the crooners — that it readily deprives us of that shade in which works of art grow, then reproaches us for taking up too much space in the sun and pretentiously getting up on the rostrum. Yet there is, truly, a huge audience in the shadows: a huge, young audience, hungry and thirsty for the sort of daring that the present time no longer supplies — and I would simply quote as an example to prove it, the twenty years that my first film, *Le Sang d'un poète*, has been showing in the same theatre in New York (a film addressed to a dozen *aficionados* and a few close friends). Little by little, our style has educated a huge anonymous audience which is utterly unlike what foreigners imagine to be the youth of France (Saint-Tropez and leather jackets). That youth is a minority which amuses itself, and sometimes rebels against the impos-

sibility of amusing itself and spending a fiver on a couple of
drinks during the holidays. It would be ridiculous to accuse
this small handful of young people of causing a scandal, and
it would be equally ridiculous to confuse it with the vast
number of young people who are attentive and curious about
the slightest rebellion against conformity. Without that
second group of young people, Picasso would not be Picasso.

October 4, 1959.

There is nowhere more abstract than a film studio because
the sets are continually changing, to such an extent that it is
impossible, every time, to recognize it and say: 'Look:
so-and-so is filming in Studio Four where I once filmed the
garage in *L'Eternel retour*.'

All of the beginning of my film takes place in Studio Four
at the Victorine Studios with a few pieces of furniture or
objects to establish the background. It is a farce, in the style
of Goldoni, on the confusions of space-time and sound. My
character who lives in an instantaneous time, different from
Earth time, and in no chronological order, instantaneously
meets the same scientist at different stages in his life. He even
succeeds in altering the professor's fate by suddenly appear-
ing in clothes from the time of Louis XV and startling the
man's young mother, who drops him on his head. Here I am
paraphrasing the story of the English ladies at the Trianon
who, instead of meeting ghosts who acted as they had in the
past, met living ghosts who talked to them and altered their
behaviour — which suggests that these ladies appeared
simultaneously during the reign of Louis XVI, astonishing
the Queen's valets as much as the Queen's valets astonished
them in 1911.

In short, I was not for a moment pretending to film a
scientific episode, but playing with modern problems as
Goldoni played around with those of his time.

My character is looking for the professor, whom he knows
to possess the secret of bringing him back to 1959. But
without the space-time farce, he would not succeed, because
it is only when the professor is too old to make use of his

discovery that he takes possession of a box of bullets which are essential to the project and brings it back to the professor at the age when he cannot yet perfect his discovery.

All of this seems very complicated when you describe it, but thanks to cinematography the pictures tell the story a thousand times better than I can, and not a single one of the technicians is ever confused by the eccentricity of it all. [Letters to François-Régis Bastide, published in *Les Lettres françaises*, N° 811, February 11, 1960].

From the young Miss France who represents Minerva to Maria Casarès who returns to her role as the Princess from *Orphée*, all the actors in my film took part with such enthuasiasm that they seem born to play the character or the figure that they portray. It is as though their gestures and speeches come directly from them, as though I am not involved and they are living each minute when they appear without being instructed by a director.

Whether or not you approve of the work, it is nonetheless true that no one in it seems to submit to the constraints of the actor's craft; and that François Périer, Jean Marais, Yul Brynner and Crémieux cannot be judged as actors, but on the same level as Mme Alec Weisweiller, her butler, Dermit or myself: as people to whom things happen and who have no theatrical craft of any sort to fall back on. I might add that the film was economical not only because of the generosity of the famous actors who gave me their collaboration, but also their instant anticipation of what I expected of them. With someone like Nicole Courcel or Françoise Christophe I did not lose a second and they gave me a depth that no mere extra could ever give. Daniel Gélin says one sentence and walks up a staircase, yet he leaves a strong impression in the memory of the spectator. Jean Marais, as the blind Oedipus who walks along, with his stick, guided by Antigone, moving his lips to speak painful and unintelligeable words, is unforgettable. The same is true of Yul Brynner: in the absence of Stroheim, he was the only person who could have carried off his role in the monumental decor of Les Baux-de-Provence.

While someone like Edouard Dermit knows nothing of the theatre, Périer knows it inside out; yet at the end of the trial scene, they move us equally, brought together by a profound simplicity, one by deliberately forgetting the craft of the stage, the other by his misunderstanding or instinctive understanding of the craft — which is the same thing.

If the names of the participants do not appear on the credits this is, firstly, because I did not wish to exploit the service that they had agreed to do me, so as to publicize the film; and secondly because some names might have deceived the public and made the audience expect more than a brief appearance by its favourite stars. [*France-Soir*, February 15, 1960].

One of the chief pleasures that I have from my film is that of proving daily that this 'modern youth which is not interested in anything' that we hear so much about, is a myth and that, while it is true that the young appear to be interested in nothing, this is perhaps because they are not given what they demand and what interests them.

The fact is that the youthful, attentive, enthusiastic audiences which go to see *Le Testament d'Orphée* take issue with those spectators who cough or dare to unwrap a sweet. Claude Mauriac writes in *Le Figaro littéraire*: 'The cinema, which was packed out, seemed for the most part full of very young people, and I was struck by their extreme concentration, their seriousness and even their solemnity. "Society", with its fine ladies and stylish gentlemen, will soon find out about this and readjust its sights.'

For it is true that the film is not a Western, or a story about adultery, or a study of juvenile delinquency. The fine ladies and stylish gentlemen of Paris can find nothing in it to sustain their appetites, and I am sure that I will gather around it, that is to say around myself, the wonderful young people of Geneva and Lausanne, symbolized by the words 'Belles Lettres', without whom I have never tried to speak in public in Switzerland. The first time, in the old days, when Ramuz and Gagnebin were alive, I went there to read *Le Secret professionnel* which was dedicated to the 'Bellettrists' of Geneva and Lausanne; and after that, often, when the hall was too full to accomodate them, I found myself addressing my audience, on my feet in the middle of these young students who were sitting crosslegged around me.

Don't imagine that I despise everyone over 20: it would be pretty ridiculous to do so at my age. But I think that, just as there are young people with old souls, there are also people who do not age and who know how to preserve their childhood within them, wide open to the marvels of the world and able to recognize dream and fantasy in whatever form it appears.

So I am speaking to the Swiss public as a whole, to warn it against the danger of seeing only the surface of my film and not understanding that it is an attempt at a self-portrait which is concerned much more with an inner likeness than with an external one, since that tells us very little about writers or painters. I learned nothing from the documentaries on Gide, Colette or Mauriac. Gide played the piano, Colette ate raw onions (in my presence) and Mauriac devoted himself to the art of being a grandfather. That is why I invented a series of actions that are linked by the processes of sleep and better designed to reveal my naked soul than to track down my habits.

I hate false solemnity and the affectation of gravity, which hide a void. The modesty of *Le Testament* is that it is not afraid of inspiring laughter and sometimes even caricaturing myself, as may happen in dreams. [*La Tribune de Genève*, March 31, 1960].

My dear Maurice Bessy,

Although I do not pretend to set myself up as an example, when it is seen as a sleep which all the spectators in a cinema experience together and share with those who sleep on their feet (that is, poets), film represents the only machine for poetry and the only means in our power to avoid the pleonasm which means reproducing forms and actions that we could not do otherwise than recognize and compare with our everyday habits.

I am fully aware that cognition demands an effort, and that recognition is much easier (this is why, for many centuries, artists have reproduced beauty instead of producing it).

It is through the force with which art departs from nature that man proves his inventive genius; and I wonder by reason of what strange weakness film might escape this rule.

If film does escape the rule, it is because of the enormous sums that it costs, which the constraints of the market oblige it to recover in the short term, instead of admitting, like other muses, that there is a need to wait until the eye and the mind of the public becomes accustomed to what Baudelaire called 'the most recent expression of beauty'.

You can imagine my gratitude when friends, known and unknown, write to me and when, at the Pagode, or in the journals of the young wave, or in the press (from *L'Humanité* to *Le Figaro*), they respect this need to express myself through the medium of cinematography, obeying no other imperative than those of my inner universe, so permitting our secret realism to take shape (to be petrified, in a sense).

A few years ago, there was an inevitable outcry against anyone who did not follow the straight and narrow. I expected nothing from this film except the joy of working in freedom. But it has brought me more: proof that it is a myth that young people 'are no longer interested in anything', and that if they appear no longer to be interested in anything, this is perhaps because they are not being given enough of what interests them.

In the long run a significant international audience is taking shape which no longer hides in cellars to see what it is being deprived of, and bit by bit a host of new little theatres is spreading, modelled on the idea of the cine-club, which is making it possible to produce films that were up to now banned by the ogre — or, if you prefer, by the terrible Minotaur which has to satisfy its immense hunger for film, stars, Oscars and raw meat. [*Le Bulletin d'information du Festival de Cannes*, N° 14, May 17, 1960].

Apart from being an inner self-portrait, the film is nothing but a translation into my own language of what I imagine to be an *Orphic initiation rite*. These initiations were similar to those of the Temple of Eleusis, and Masonic initiations are a sort of decadent version of this ceremony that went as far as threats of death (Minerva and her pseudo-death). Even Descartes, someone for whom I do not hide my dislike and whom I class among the redcoated gentlemen of the Hunt who pursue poets, was interested in secret ceremonies and obscure rituals, and a Rosecrucian.

However, in opposition to the closed circle of Descartes or Voltaire and the Encyclopedists, I support the half-open circle of a Pascal or a Jean-Jacques Rousseau, despite the tedium and naïve grandiloquence that Jean-Jacques piles on.

I am the model of an anti-intellectual and my film confirms it. At first, I imagined it in twilight, the half-sleep that allows the obscurity within us to be smuggled into the light, as it were surreptitiously: slipping past the noses of the intellectual customs which control the export of illicit merchandise. Then, in the long run, commercial difficulties and the problem of finding a small sum of money (which is a very suspect proposition to those who invest large ones) took me further and further away from the object of my enterprise, and this object, with distance, became as incomprehensible to me, as foreign, even as stupid as it was to those wheelers and dealers who claim to know the public and understand what it wants.

It was at this point that my entirely new team made me feel ashamed at letting myself be defeated by the judgement of intelligence (the poet's worst enemy). Because this very simple crew of electricians and technicians found it entirely normal to make huge efforts for episodes about which I was within a hair's breadth of feeling ashamed. These men represented the wonderful innocence that I was starting to lose.

I did not dare play my own part: they made the effort to persuade me that no one else could stand in for me. In short, it was through respect for the enthusiasm and courage of the crew, and gratitude for their confidence and their kindness, that I rediscovered the childhood that I had lost. In a sense, I had aged during the exhausting search for money which producers were falling over one another to offer me, until they had a look at my screenplay and script.

A fine work of cinematography has no connection with ink and it is important to mistrust the appeal of a story that falls to pieces on the screen.

When people asked me: 'What do you expect from this film?', I answered: 'I have too deep a joy in making it to expect or hope for anything else from it.' Since then, some weeks of full houses — full of young people — have brought me a different feeling of joy: that of having evidence that these 'young people who are interested in nothing' are a myth, and that if they appear not to be interested in anything, it may be because they are not offered what they want and what interests them.

While exegesis is a muse (and, more precisely, a German muse), there is a danger in critical analysis. A poet has a duty to accept what his inner darkness dictates, as a sleeper accepts a dream. And with no greater supervision than in a dream. So it is clear that he says far more than he thinks he is saying, and it is right to explore his unconscious work, just as Freud and Jung look for people's real personality in their dreams. But there is still a danger of searching too hard and, just as psychoanalysts may do, manufacturing relations that fall back into the error of intellectuals. This is what I unfortunately often see in the articles where young critics are most favourable towards my work. I am quite happy to be an unconscious sex maniac or a criminal, but it is ridiculous to feign art when I avoid it and to overload with signs and symbols a work that stakes its claim to nobility on the fact that it never has recourse to them.

Le Testament d'Orphée has nothing to do with dreams. It borrows the mechanism of dreaming, that is all. For the reality of dreams places us in situations and events that do not surprise us, absurdly splendid though they are. We submit to them without the slightest surprise, and if the splendour becomes tragic, we have no chance of escaping, except by waking up, over which we have no control. Film allows a large number of people to dream the same dream together and this dream, which is not a dream, but a transcendent reality, must not allow the spectators to wake up, that is to say, to leave our universe for their own, because then they would be as bored as people to whom we tell our dreams. This is where the problem starts: the slightest over-long passage, drop in tension or lapse of interest, and the spectator will escape from the collective hypnosis; and this one escape is liable to prove contagious and lead to others. This is what I was afraid of and was very surprised to find, from the accounts I have been given, that my houses are attentive and do not, either voluntarily or by accident, resist the fakir that a cinema screen must become through its light and the images that unfold on it.

It amuses me when people reproach me for using tricks and special effects: not to do so would be to deprive films of their main talent, which is that of being able to show the unreal with the demonstrability of realism. One wonders why I should give up an asset that cinematography alone possesses; and, in that case, why I should not turn to books or the theatre, with the exception, naturally, of the subterfuges and stratagems that can prevent the theatre from becoming a tedious imitation of life.

Our age tends to confuse boredom with seriousness, and to suspect anything that does not remind it that it is a grown-up, ashamed of amusing itself. This was summed up by the famous remark that Picasso and I heard from a spectator about the outrage over *Parade*: 'If I had known that it was so silly, I would have brought the children.' But don't think I despise films that record real life, or at least those which, thanks to a kind of genius, succeed in pretending that they are taken from real life. The bedroom scene, in *A bout de souffle*, and the interview with the psychiatrist in *Les Quatre cents coups*, are unforgettable masterpieces. I should not wish anyone to believe, for anything in the world, that I am offering myself as an example and asking to be followed. *Le Testament* activates a field that is peculiar to me and which would be tiresome, were it to become a genre. I am a poet who hates poetic style and language, but who can only express himself in poetry, that is to say by transmuting quantities into numerals and thought into action. If I made a film of *Les Parents terribles*, that was because there was a problem for me to solve: filming a play without changing anything, but in such a way that it was metamorphozed into cinematography. The problem I had to solve in *Le Testament* was to turn immodesty upside down, by undressing myself of my body so that I could exhibit my naked soul.

Alain Resnais writes to me: 'What a lesson in freedom you give all of us!' — a remark of which I am proud. It is no doubt this freedom that our critics describe as childishness. Do they, our critics, know how to walk lightly on the surface of deep waters? Do they, in their passion for modernism, know that people will soon smile at the knights of space as they do at the first motorists, hidden behind their glasses and their fur coats? Do they know what is implied in being a judge? Do they know that the really fine science is to forget one's learning? Resnais, Bresson, Doniol-Valcroze, Franju, Truffaut, Langlois and you, critics, and you, numberless young people who write letters to me that I lovingly preserve: how can I thank you all for consoling me in my long solitude and giving me the courage to live?

PS A journalist, after exhausting me with pertinent and impertinent questions, asked me: 'Where does Cégeste take you at the end of your film?' — to which I had to reply: 'He takes me where you are not.'

But this departure should not be confused with death. I leave this universe for another, and I should like to leave it one day murmuring what was shouted by a gentlemen after a performance at the Théâtre de l'Avenue: 'I didn't understand a thing. I demand my money back.'

Dates

Talleyrand said: 'Treason is a matter of dates.' Success also. It is probable that, unlike my other films, *Le Testament* has come at the right time. *Le Sang d'un poète* opposed surrealism when that was all the rage. *La Belle et la Bête* arrived in the midst of Italian neo-realism, *L'Aigle à deux têtes* in the midst of the psychoanalytical period, *Orphée* before *Orfeu Negro*, and, after the unqualified success of Jean Marais in *Le Bossu*, a re-run of *Ruy Blas*, which shocked people by its Westernism, would no doubt prove a triumph. After *Le Testament*, we might rediscover Dermit's marvellous performance in *Les Enfants terribles*. But where are the films of yesteryear? [*Cahiers du cinéma*, N° 108, June 1960].

La Voix humaine

Paisà is a masterpiece in which a people expresses itself through a man and a man through a people. I entrusted *La Voix humaine* to Roberto Rossellini because he has charm and ties himself down with none of the rules that govern cinematography.

In twenty-five takes, amounting to a total of 1200 metres of film, he has shot a cruel documentary on a woman's suffering. In it, Anna Magnani reveals a soul and a face without make-up.

This documentary might be entitled 'Woman devoured by a girl' or 'The telephone as an instrument of torture'. Anna Magnani acted in Italian. She will dub herself in French. [*La Revue du cinéma*, N° 7, Summer 1947].

Ruy Blas

Ruy Blas is the opposite of *La Belle et la Bête* and *La Voix humaine*. It is a film that is active, to the greatest possible degree, a drama in which the mechanics are similar to those of vaudeville. Indeed, everything depends on the misunderstandings that arise from the resemblance between Ruy Blas and Don César.

Shining heroes live out a hare-brained intrigue in the midst of an invented Spain, a veritable catafalque, an inquisitorial pyre, a scaffold for kings. I entrusted Pierre Billon with the task of moving them, and Georges Wakhévitch with that of imprisoning them in an entanglement of doors. Michel Kelber's lighting completes this architectural structure. [*La Revue du cinéma*, N° 7, Summer 1947].

Ruy Blas, inspired by *La Reine d'Espagne*, a play by Henri de Latouche, was written very rapidly by Victor Hugo, in the way that one might paint a set. There are some implausible elements when you read it carefully. Film work demands rigorous plotting, and this was not easy. Moreover, the theatre made it impossible for Hugo to make use of the physical likeness between Ruy Blas and Don César: it is mentioned, but you do not believe in it. On the other hand, this likeness becomes the very basis of the film. The same actor is to play both parts. This is the excuse for a comic and tragic misunderstanding, which entirely accords with the style of the work. The most serious problem was de-versifying. But Hugo, despite his huge sweep, does not overlook details, which almost entirely take over our dialogues and give the rhythm. The Hugolian wave rolls from beginning to end, giving its sound. Everyone knows it. The main thing is for the ear to pick it up.

The whole atmosphere of the film should be that of El Greco on one side and Goya on the other. The courtiers in Madrid are black and funereal, but with that supreme elegance of the characters in 'The Burial of the Count d'Orgaz'. When the film shows the Queen and Casilda, Goya takes over. The Queen has basset hounds in her room. In the streets, during her escape, the streets are walls, blocks of shadow and moonlight.

Spain is falling apart. Everything is crumbling. Grass grows between the paving stones. The *alguaciles* are not police, but henchmen. In the palace there is an incredible degree of laxity. The only thing that remains untouched is the ritual around the Queen. The palace in Madrid has the appearance of a large, empty hotel after an occupation. Here and there, you can see a magnificent piece of furniture. It is warm. Through the window, you can hear the tempestuous music of a guitar. This is Seville, or Grenada, this is Madrid. (There is no question of a particular historical style. What we have here is the imaginary Spain of the Romantic movement).

The sets for *Ruy Blas* will be in openwork, latticed wood, in scaffolds and catafalques, so that they reveal the void suggested by black velvets.

In this way the action will be described rather than real, and the white light of the arc-lamps will sculpt the sets in the style of Victor Hugo's admirable drawings. [*Paris*, Paul Morihien, 1948].

L'Eternel retour

For a long time I have cherished the dream of taking the theme of Tristan and Yseult, and setting it in our own time. There were insurmountable obstacles to this in the theatre or in a book. But, living amid the work of the astonishing fantasy factories of cinematography, I realized that film was the only medium capable of achieving a balance between the real and the unreal, in order to elevate a modern story to the status of myth. It was thanks to André Paulvé's confidence in

me and the friendship of Jean Delannoy that I was able to try
and solve the problem.

Indeed, in a film, the text counts for little. It is important
to make it invisible. The eye's primacy over the ear means
that the poet has to tell the story in silence and to put the
images together, anticipating the slightest degree of distanc-
ing or relief in each one.

What would I have become without Delannoy, who
wanted to get on my wavelength and asked me to join him in
the cutting and montage; or without Roger Hubert, who
filmed through my eyes and my heart?

I am taking advantage of these few lines to thank the firm,
the actors and Georges Auric, whose wonderful music cut
the last thread that still held us to the ground; and, from the
set designer to the most junior technician, the whole, incom-
parable crew of *L'Eternel retour*. [*Aspects*, N° 1, November 5,
1943].

I have been very amused by some articles published in
London which accused *L'Eternel retour* of being Germanic in
inspiration because of its blond heroes and, I suppose,
because of Wagner's opera. Yet *Tristan*, paraphrased in
L'Eternel retour, is a work that belongs as much to England as
to France. Yseult sets sail on the Thames to join the dying
Tristan; and you can no more imagine Tristan and Yseult as
brunettes than you can imagine Carmen as a blonde.

I belong to the generation that fought against Wagnerism.
I am pleased to say that I have now reached the age when
you lay down your arms. I let myself be carried away on
Wagner's waves and allowed his magic to work. So it was not
through senseless anti-Germanism, but out of respect for his
work that I did not even consider using it.

There are very few great stories of love in which the couple
triumphs. *Tristan* is the model. I wanted to harmonize a
legend, the most famous of all, with the rhythm of our age,
and to prove that Nietzsche's *éternel retour* could be translated
by the repetition throughout the centuries of coincidences,

surprises, obstacles and dreams which set up a storyline that other people relive without even realising it.

I persist in saying and repeating: I am not concerned with Fantasy and Poetry. They have to take me by ambush. My itinerary does not allow for them. If I guess that this or that shaded spot is more likely than another to conceal them, I cheat, because it happens that an open road in full sunlight often provides better cover for them.

This is why I am as keen to live in Belle's family as in the Beast's castle (in *La Belle et la Bête*). This is why the appearance or style of the fantastic is more important to me than the fantastic itself.

This is why, among others, the episode of the sedan chairs in the courtyard, an episode that has no connection with fantasy, is in my opinion more significant than any trick in the castle.

In *Le Sang d'un poète*, the blood which flows across the film has upset some critics. What is the point, they wonder, in deliberately disgusting and shocking us? The flowing blood forces us to turn away and prevents us from enjoying what is original and inventive — by this, they mean the passage through the mirror, the moving statue and the beating heart. But, I ask you, what is the link between each one of these tremors that wake the critics up, except the flowing blood that gives my film its title? They only feel the bumps. This is what excites them, makes them fidget and sends them running from place to place and from one opinion to another.

In *L'Eternel retour*, the lovers' castle seems to them appropriate for poetry, but the garage of the brother and sister, inappropriate: they condemn it. Strange folly, because it is precisely in the garage that the poetry functions best.

In reality, in understanding the abandonment of the brother and sister, in their innate and, as it were, organic misunderstanding of grace, you touch directly on poetry and I come close to the terrible mysteries of love.

As far as cinematography is concerned, I think that the progress of its soul is not connected with the progress of its machines. On the contrary, it seems that wealth and simplicity have deprived the work of drama and are in some way extinguishing its powers of hypnosis.

This is our last hope in a country where the electricity fails, the lights are unreliable, and the microphones and equipment look like an old streetcar. Our imagination and that of the technicians, which is superb, have to make up for the deficiencies of the material. This forces us to work hard and deprives us of any opportunity for laziness.

In fact, I would go further. Cinematography, because of the immediate returns that it demands, will become more and more like the large publishing houses that descend to asking their authors to write the novels that they want to sell.

This is why I am turning to 16mm film, a perfect weapon with which the poet can hunt for beauty, alone, free and with his 'shot-gun' camera on his shoulder.

A contradiction (and one of which America offers some extraordinary examples) will bring these modest undertakings within the reach of all.

I myself have just made a film of this kind in my garden. In it, I rediscovered the sharpness and total freedom of my youth, when I knew nothing of the craft and invented it to my own ends.

Between ourselves, I prefer this means of expression to those massive projects that weigh us down with endless responsibilities and employ too many people. In addition to our official works, we must have these marginal ones, these secret works that have always been the hidden wealth of the country which glories in Rimbaud.

L'Eternel retour is a film over which I exercised only friendly supervision. Delannoy directed it. I thank the whole team; and Madeleine Sologne, whose hairstyle I invented without knowing that Veronica Lake was inventing the same at the same time in Hollywood; and Jean Marais who, in the last reel, reaches the greatest heights to which an actor can aspire.

Cinematography is only fifty years old. This is very young for a muse. It is still taking its first steps. In my opinion, it is on the way to becoming the complete art, *par excellence*, a popular theatre from which nothing is absent: music, dance, words, Greek masks (close-up), the whisper that hundreds of ears can hear and everything that goes to make up drama. But if it is to be used correctly, it is essential for authors not only not to despise it, but to dedicate themselves to it body and soul. Paper, film and the uncomfortable earth on which we live will all soon pass away. Human pride should remember this, and we should not be afraid to express ourselves through images, on the grounds that they are less durable than the written word. Nothing ages better than a good film.

La Princesse de Clèves

Mme de La Fayette's story is quite simply an orgy of purity. It was hard to get a very free younger generation to accept this. Excessive freedom, the impossibility of disobedience, and the weariness that results from that, may perhaps allow them to understand the strange attitude of a woman who asks her husband to defend her against the impulses of her heart.

Apart from some liberties which were essential to translate the plot of a long black-and-white film, we have kept the quality of the vigorous style that the novelist used, in contrast to the flourishes of her age. Our hope is that the spiritual nobility and moral behaviour of the characters, which correspond to the sort of sumptuous armour provided by their costumes, will carry the audience down through the ages and have the same kind of appeal, perhaps, as we enjoy at the spectacle of the discovery of distant and unknown worlds.

I congratulate Jean Delannoy because, instead of dressing the present up in the costumes of the past, he has given contemporary meaning to a dead time, as foreign to our own as the fauna and flora of the stars. [*L'Avant-Scène Cinéma*, N° 3, April 15, 1961].

IV   Unpublished Synopses

Orphée

The poets' café is a rendez-vous for young writers and a host of artists and snobs whose feelings for Orphée are a mixture of admiration and jealousy.

Orphée is the official poet hallowed by fame. That day, his attention is drawn by a very elegant woman, referred to as the Princess. But a fight breaks out, between some young people and Cégeste, a very drunk poet whom the Princess tries in vain to extricate from the mêlée. The confusion is increased by the arrival of the police and, trying to flee, Cégeste is wounded by two motorcyclists who career into the square.

The Princess shouts across to Orphée, asking him to accompany her to the hospital where she is taking the young man, so that he can serve as a witness. But on the way, Orphée notices that the young man is dead and that the car has left the town. The motorcyclists catch up with the car and it stops in front of a chalet on the summit of a hill. Orphée follows the Princess and is amazed to see her revive Cégeste and lead him through the mirror in the room which they have entered, and then disappear. Orphée rushes after them, but crashes against the glass and is knocked out.

When he comes back to his senses, he is alone on the deserted hill. The chalet has vanished. Heurtebise, the Princess's chauffeur — who is none other than Death — is dozing in the car. He takes Orphée back home where his wife, Eurydice, was worried by his absence and by rumours that Orphée has caused the disappearance of Cégeste who cannot be found after the incident at the café.

But Orphée is entirely preoccupied by the strange events he has witnessed and by thoughts of the Princess. He neglects Eurydice to listen to messages on the radio of Heurtebise's car, which he anxiously tries to unravel.

Ordered by the police commissioner to present himself, to answer the charges against him, Orphée meets the Princess, but tries in vain to reach her. He does not know that every night the Princess emerges from the mirror in his room and comes towards him . . . Eurydice is expecting a child. In despair at being abandoned by her husband, she decides to go and share her grief with her former friends, the Bacchantes, who hate Orphée. But on her way the young woman is knocked down by the motorcyclists of Death and carried off in her turn to the mysterious realm of the Beyond.

Informed of what has happened by Heurtebise, Orphée finally gives up listening to the messages — which were sent out by Cégeste — to follow Heurtebise to the realm of Death, with the help of gloves which allow him to pass through mirrors. In this way, they go through a desolate region and finally reach the Palace where the Supreme Tribunal judges Death, who is guilty of having acted without orders. Here all secrets are revealed: the Princess's love for Orphée, and the love that Heurtebise feels, without knowing it, for Eurydice.

Orphée is allowed to take his wife back, on condition that he never looks at her again. Heurtebise will help them to abide by this clause: they soon understand how difficult it will be. Feeling that she will never again be able to recover Orphée's love, Eurydice tries to die for the second time by forcing her husband to look at her. At last she succeeds and disappears for ever.

Almost at the same moment, the poets and the Bacchantes burst into the poet's house, still accusing him of having carried off their friend Cégeste. Heurtebise argues in defence of Orphée, but a shot rings out and the young man falls, killed instantly. Taking the place of the police who have arrived on the spot, the motorcyclists of Death help Heurtebise to get Orphée into the Princess's car.

Death and Cégeste are waiting for them in the intermediate region. But, sacrificing her love to that of the living, the Princess orders her aides, Heurtebise and Cégeste, to bring Orphée back to life at Eurydice's side.

An Episode from 'The Life of Coriolan: or It Goes Without Saying'

The feudal system had not yet acquired its final form in 1292. Behind the scenes, the landed nobility was engaged in a struggle against the nobility of the royal court. The resulting wars, called 'The Wars of the Princes', harmed the people without enriching the nobles. We shall try to present one of these wars to the audience, while pointing out that the characters are fictitious and bear no relation to historical reality, except the character of Coriolan — it goes without saying.

Coriolan

Held captive in the prisons of Tékalémit, realm of the illustrious Popof family, Coriolan escapes.

In his castle of Tékalémit, Count Popof, guarded by his sleigh dogs, is consulting a treatise on hunting for eagles.

The luxury of these feudal times is beyond human imagining. The number of servants is known to have been uncountable. Not one of these great nobles would have demeaned himself, in turning the page of a book, to wet his finger on his own tongue.

The Count has misplaced his spectacles. He calls for his steward. The steward thinks that it is for tongue-service. He is wrong. Mad with fury, Count Popof strikes him a savage blow.

His anger is fearful.

But he calms down and examines the sky. He is looking for eagles.

Coriolan, free, takes revenge on one of his foes.

Meanwhile Count Popof sets out to hunt eagles.

Thinking he sees one, he fires. Heavens! A young dog falls at his feet.

Count Popof, who loves dogs, laments.

Coriolan has heard his cries. He ceases to whip his foe and runs towards the sound of lamentation.

(His enemy is bleeding. Silent shot.)

Popof hears a suspicious noise. He listens, but when he looks, the dog has become a young woman.

Coriolan emerges from the bushes. He sees the Count. The young girl is transformed into his enemy.

He approaches and, taking advantage of the Count's terror and amazement, seizes his dead enemy from him and vanishes.

The Count watches him leave, stupified.

While he is abducting his enemy, the man once again becomes a young woman. Coriolan runs and sets her down on a lawn.

It is a croquet lawn. The players, furious, threaten him.

Brave Coriolan is frightened by their unknown weapons. He makes his escape.

A player addresses the ball, using the young woman's head. The players rush forward and tie her down with the croquet hoops.

Horror! The young woman has again turned into Coriolan's enemy.

A player takes Coriolan's enemy by the head. The head comes off in his hands.

The terrified players watch what is happening.

Count Popof has gone back to the hunt. Looking for eagles, he suddenly sees the young woman and Coriolan's enemy embracing at the window of the Baillif's house.

He fires.

Coriolan's enemy falls out of the window.

The Count is rooted to the spot.

The young woman comes out of the house in tears, throws herself on the body of Coriolan's enemy and covers it with kisses.

The Count is about to flee, but Coriolan calls and touches him on the shoulder. The Count is petrified. Coriolan turns him round, snatches off his hat and beard, symbol of his power. Then he puts a rope round his neck. The defeated Count dies.

Pas de Chance

I intend to make a film for a wide international audience.

My method will be to use gags: that is to say, every image should make up a whole and an inventive idea that leads on to the next.

Here is an outline of the subject:

A boastful young sailor comes out of prison in Calvi and rejects Rachel, a chick of indeterminate age, who was expecting to follow him when he was freed. He goes back to the small provincial town where he lives with his mother and sister, his brother and a young cousin who is in love with him (even though she knows all about him) and would like to marry him. This young cousin has refused an offer of marriage from a journalist who started in the provinces and has just made his name in Paris.

'Pas de chance' — 'No Luck' — so-called after the tattoo on his chest, finds a job at a printers' and dreams of being the gangster that he boasts of having been in Corsica and that he boasted of having been in the Navy while he was serving his time in Corsica.

Letter after letter from Rachel. He burns them. One night, she arrives after announcing that she is on her way. '*Pas de chance*' is waiting for her near the station. He is shocked by her flashy clothes and make-up and the idea that people will pass comments on them. He invites her to 'talk things over' at the printing-works: he has the key.

Their discussion reaches such a point that he hits her and accidentally kills her with a pile of proofs. He drags her outside. He props her up against a post. He feels faint and leans against an old, peeling poster. He leaves the print of his bloody hand and, in the middle, his victim's lipstick which he had kept after reducing her to silence during their quarrel.

He returns home, goes to bed and, the next morning, intoxicated by the idea of becoming 'famous', amazing his family, the small town and the world, goes to the police station to give himself up.

Three false killers have already given themselves up, acting according to the familiar behaviour pattern of pseudo-criminals. The police refuse to believe him, particularly as he is known as a braggart and a megalomaniac, and because when he describes the crime he exaggerates it, saying that he committed it with a knife.

(One of the most striking features of the film will be that the real scenes and those that are described, or lies, will be seen and shot from different angles.)

At home, he asserts his guilt. They refuse to believe him. He goes to confession: secret of the confessional, etc.

People tease him by calling him 'the killer'. Every night he follows the trail of the crime and stands in front of the shops at the time of the murder.

One day, worn out, he goes for a swim in the river. Coming out, he finds himself confronted by a young man sitting on the bank. The man sees Pas de chance rising out of the water. He is the journalist, who has been sent to report by a leading newspaper.

The journalist saw the poster, tore it off and took it away: he has evidence. He tells him. Pas de chance is delirious! At last, he will be *believed*, and accused properly. But he is wrong: the journalist is going to save him despite himself. He does not want anyone to say that he only turned him in to get rid of a rival. He protects him in order to force him to make the girl happy. What rival? He loves only his crime. He loves only that *hour of his life*.

The film will be made up of the thousand obstacles which prevent him from being caught and his rejection of happiness. It doesn't matter to him. He only wants *that*.

Mother, sister, brother, fiancée, etc.

He will be betrayed by the brother, a low type who is jealous of the role that the journalist's revelation gives his brother in their home.

The journalist thinks that Pas de chance has stolen the evidence from him. It is the brother. Chase to catch up with him. Too late. For one last night, he retraces his stations of the cross and confesses to a prostitute who begs him to keep quiet. At the hour of the murder, he arrives in front of the shop. At the same moment, the young cousin seizes his hands to drag him away from there and the hands of the police land on his shoulders. He asks to be allowed a moment to himself. He wants to enjoy his triumph. *At last, he experiences love.* He is free. He finds his own peace. Pas de chance's peace. The culmination of his dream. The girl and the journalist are linked by fate. She loved a phantom. They will each find their own fate.

It would be impossible to narrate such a film without the work of the cutting-room. Indeed, it only exists through the contrast of lies — by this luck that is ill-luck — and all the back-to-front obstacles of the hunted man — 'the man who cannot succeed in being hunted'.

The start, in jail, is very important for me, as well as the scenes of the mother and sons, of the police interrogations, the ridiculing of the man, etc., which I have not mentioned along the way. [*Empreintes*, N° 7-8, May-June-July 1950, Brussels, Editions 'L'Ecran du Monde'].

The Gaslight: A Farcical Comedy

A young man and young woman have a dance routine. The young man adores the young woman. She is an impossible character and turns him down because she considers him too simple and sweet-natured. Her mother urges her to marry a very ill-mannered impresario whom she rejects with scorn.

One day, after their performance, they join the audience to watch the act of a famous fakir. The girl is sceptical and makes a scene. The fakir invites her to take part in an experiment. The young man shouts to him to hypnotize her and order her to be sweet and charming until the next day.

The girl challenges him to do it. He puts her into a trance and the audience sees a calm, modest young woman come down from the stage. The fakir invites them to return the next day, when he will wake her up.

On leaving the music hall, the fakir is killed when his car hits a gaslight at the end of the avenue with the music hall.

It is impossible to bring the girl out of her trance. Journalists come; they take her to see doctors. They make fun of the young man, who is complaining because she has become so charming. Her mother once more urges her to marry the rich impresario. Submissively, she agrees. Scenes with the man who becomes mad with fury and, bit by bit, becomes as aggressive as she used to be. Their characters have been reversed.

One evening, their car hits the gaslight where the fakir was killed. The girl comes round and hits the young man, who does the same to her. Now both of them are ill-natured.

Life becomes so utterly unbearable that one evening, after a row in the car, the man decides to have done with it and deliberately drives the car into the same gaslight.

They lose consciousness in the wrecked car.

The screen shows a vast flower-lined road down which they are walking in a bridal dress and morning coat. They walk away, hand in hand, getting smaller and smaller. When they have become mere dots in the distance, we hear bells and a voice, vaguely shouting: 'I give them a fortnight.'

The picture clouds and changes to a hospital room. The beds are adjacent. He is in one, she next to him, and the doctor is saying: 'I give them a fortnight' — to the weeping mother.

They come out of the anaesthetic. Under their bandages, they look at each other . . . smile and hold hands.

La Ville Maudite

A boy has been driven out of the provincial town where he
lives because he was brought up as an orphan in a family and
seems to want to gain some ascendancy over the daughter of
the house. In face of the family's growing hostility, he rebels,
runs away and lives by theft and doing odd jobs. He still
thinks about the girl and about gaining revenge. He comes
out of the forest near the town and hides in a woodsman's
hut where, at one time, he used to play at gypsies with the
girl. There he comes across some children from the town who
are boy scouts camping in the woods. He surprises them,
gains their admiration and becomes the secret leader of their
gang. He trains them to hate miserly and wicked families.
Back home, they keep their eyes open, nose around and
bring reports back to him. (Think of Savonarola and his
young children).

One day the girl's little brother is caught in the act while
searching through her things. She questions him and learns
that a boy is the gang leader. She decides to go secretly to
find out about him. She does so and comes face to face with
the former tearaway. He has turned into a handsome youth.
Involuntarily, she is attracted to him and begins secretly to
bring him food — tries to persuade him to leave. Eventually
he succeeds in convincing her of the ugliness of the small
town where she is wasting her life and wins her over to his
side.

Bit by bit, the girl realizes that he is getting involved in an
affair of anonymous letters, etc. She wants to save the boy —
begs him to give up his revenge. He accepts, if she will run
away with him. She refuses, terrified by the prospect of a
rootless existence.

He threatens her. Furious, she denounces him, he is
arrested. Scandal. Trial. The townspeople are so vile that the
girl realizes she loves the boy and wants to save him. (He
thinks he hates her). So she starts to play the same game as
he did, ganging the children together, and succeeds in

exposing two or three families. This leads her to her own family which is terrified of what might come out. The fact that the letters, etc., go on during the boy's imprisonment takes some of the blame off him. The authorities look for the real culprit, or his accomplice, and are led to the girl. She confesses and insults them and the town. She is imprisoned. The trial and their relationship in prison (see Stendhal's *La Chartreuse de Parme*) would make up a large part of the film. Both are saved by the children whose evidence is such that people are forced to realize that they were acting on the side of justice. They are let out, mobbed and acclaimed by the children who want to stay with them for good. They set up a home (like a modern charity), with the children forming a kind of youth camp under the leadership of our heroes. Marriage surrounded by the children.

This is the outline of a film about savagery, woodland and small town life which would symbolize the victory of youthful purity over corruption. The children should also play a major part.

Three scandalous stories among the leading families would be brought into this work of savage purity.

The film would have the merit of bearing on all these contemporary themes, with elements of passionate love and bourgeois tragedy. Refer to the business of the families in Lyons.

La Vénus d'Ille (from a Story by Mérimée)

A disturbed young woman is being cared for in an asylum near Perpignan. The doctor meets her father in a large garden under the Canigou. The doctor has come there in an attempt to discover the cause of his patient's madness from her father, the archaeologist M. de Puygarrig. She keeps on repeating: 'She hugged him, hugged him in her arms', staring wildly and pointing at something. The doctor cannot hope to cure her unless he knows the details of a very vague

story which is gradually being turned into a myth. M. de
Puygarrig and the doctor talk, sitting on a bench behind
which stands an empty pedestal. 'Here,' M. de Puygarrig
says, tapping the pedestal with his cane, 'that is where she
was.' 'Don't get upset,' says the doctor, 'tell me about it . . . '
And the film starts.

It begins in M. de Peyrehorade's estate, not far from that
of M. de Puygarrig. A wealthy and unusual house. Magnifi-
cent garden. (All these fantastic events will take place in
broad sunlight, with a few heavy, but brief downpours).

M. de Peyrehorade's son, Georges, is a poet who has not
written anything. He is a poet who is unaware of being one,
and this condition causes him great unease. The family
house and garden are just a family house and garden to his
mother and father, but he can only see the mystery behind
them. The wind often blows in Ille. Doors slam, windows fly
open, curtains flap and wrap themselves around you, the
furniture creaks and branches grasp at you as you walk by.
Georges thinks he is being persecuted by the hatred of the
objects around him. Everything causes him anxiety and
terror. His only comfort is his neighbour, Julie de Puygarrig,
the archaeologist's daughter, whom he loves, who loves him
and whom he meets secretly on the road outside, because his
father hates Puygarrig and despises him for losing his money
in research and fruitless excavations. Georges would never
dare speak about Julie or his love at home.

The Peyrehorades have a tennis court, of which M. de
Peyrehorade is very proud; he wants to embellish it with a
little antique-style amphitheatre. Work has started on the
building and he is directing it. The workmen are digging and
shovelling. In the course of this, the spade of one of the men
(Jean Coll) hits something and makes a noise like a gong.
The statue is discovered. M. de Peyrehorade is wild with
delight at the idea of scoring over his neighbour and shouts:
'An antique, an antique!' Very carefully, they dig out a black
hand and arm. Georges and the workmen are terrified. M. de
Peyrehorade tells them they are idiots and picks up the
shovel himself. The Venus is dug out. It tips over and breaks

Jean Coll's leg. First incident. The statue. A splendid Venus, made of copper, black, shiny, covered in grass, moss, grey mould, its enamel eyes wide open, with a malicious look on its face, holding its folded garments with one hand and playing *morra* with the other — its fingers (the thumb and first two fingers) held out — Its posture is similar to that of the *morra* player known by the name Germanicus.

(*Morra* is still played in Italy. One player has to guess quickly how many fingers the other player is pointing when he stretches out his hand).

News of the find quickly spreads. M. de Puygarrig cannot contain himself. He is eaten up with jealousy. He must see the Idol: this is the name which everyone calls the Venus. The Idol, the Idol! Throughout Roussillon they speak fearfully about the Idol. The workmen cross themselves. She broke Jean Coll's leg!

M. de Peyrehorade lectures his wife and daughter. He has found a treasure! Only one man will realize its significance: Puygarrig. Hatred vanishes, replaced by pride and the desire to show off the Venus. He embraces Puygarrig. He goes to fetch him and takes him to the garden. And, while Georges and Julie are hiding together, he shows him the statue, on a plinth formerly occupied by a plaster faun. Puygarrig is astonished. The statue is a gem of Roman art. Magnifying glass. Examination. The inscription *Cave a Mantem*. Argument. One of them translates: 'Beware him who loves you'; the other: 'Beware if she loves you'. They discuss the game of *morra*. On its arm, the trace of a bracelet and the word *Turbul*. The rest is obliterated. Meaning of *Turbul*. Venus who causes disturbance, agitation — or the start of a place name?

The two old men have forgotten their long-standing hostility. They are too worked up and too excited by the problem of the Venus.

In this way, the Puygarrigs are soon welcome at the Peyrehorade's. In the evening, Julie and Georges find themselves on the bench next to the pedestal of the statue, with the statue leaning forward above them with its dark, cruel little head. Sometimes they amuse themselves by playing

morra (the game of *morra*). One evening, Georges and Julie
promise to marry, in spite of their parents. That evening,
they kiss and embrace. *As they are walking away, the statue slowly
turns its head and seems to follow them with its eyes.* (The day
before, a drop of water fell on Julie. It had been raining. The
water fell off the statue's fingers). Confession to the parents.
Peyrehorade's fury. Of course! He has opened his door to
ruin, to this affair! Row between the two old men. 'Take
care,' Puygarrig tells him. 'Your son Georges is a poet who
does not write verse. If he did, it would not be so serious. But
I know him better than you do. Ask your wife who is terrified
for him. He loves Julie. Julie loves him. Let's marry them.
He needs the support of a love that will take him away from
his fantasies, a simple wife, children . . . ' 'But you are
penniless!' 'My daughter is worth a fortune!' and so on. 'We
must wait. This is a passing fancy, Georges doesn't know
what it means to be in love.'

One day, in Perpignan, Georges is at the Platanes where
he sees an elegant woman coming down the steps. She stops.
She is holding a scarf and her dress. Her pose is the same as
the statue's. She is wearing a broad gold bracelet. (The same
actress plays the part of the statue and of the lady). He also
stops, amazed. When he tries to follow her, she vanishes.

When he gets back to Peyrehorade, Georges is preoccu-
pied and forgets his meetings under the statue. He shuts
himself up in his room. Julie is sitting alone on the bench.
Jean Coll, whose leg has healed, without seeing her,
approaches over the tennis court with a friend and throws a
stone at the statue. There is a sound like a gong which
startles Julie. She sits up and gives a cry. Another cry. The
stone has ricochetted off the statue and hit Coll's head.
Georges, who was by his window, runs down. Jean Coll's
anger. Julie's tears. Row between Georges and his father.
The Venus was not meant to be in their house. The father
rows, while Puygarrig laughs: 'Take it to my place.' Julie:
'Oh, no!' Mme de Peyrehorade thinks the children and Coll
are right. The Idol is evilly disposed towards them. M. de
Peyrehorade can only think of one thing: they risked damag-

ing a masterpiece. With Puygarrig, they go and gently try to erase the mark left by the stone.

More encounters with the mysterious lady in Perpignan. Once, with her head bent, she comes round a street corner; another time, with her head bent, she disappears into a doorway; on yet another occasion, she vanishes beneath the Castillet. Georges, who only happens to notice her by chance, cannot discover where she has gone. His sinks into a more and more sombre mood and Julie is in despair.

One day in Perpignan, the mysterious lady is sitting on a bench in the Platanes. Georges can restrain himself no longer and goes up to her. She answers quite freely. She tells him to sit down. She knows him very well by sight. She is Italian and has rented the large estate at Prades, further down the road from Peyrehorade, between Ille and the sea. She invites Georges to visit her. Then she walks away and disappears.

On their bench, Georges confesses these meetings to Julie and tells her of the lure that the Italian woman has for him. He is not in love, but he is attracted, maddened, fascinated by her. He wants the wedding to take place as soon as possible.

Julie, touched by his honesty, tells Georges's mother about the Italian woman and asks her to hasten the marriage. The mother will persuade M. de Peyrehorade. She has taken a liking to Julie.

Georges, meanwhile, is restless and goes to Prades. It is a huge, very strange estate. The house is very old, very bizarre and quite impossible to understand from the outside, set in a forest of eucalyptus trees, oleanders and shrubs. A stream courses through the park alongside huge planations of vines, peaches, tomatoes and flowers. In the distance, you can sense the sea. He pushes the park gate open. He goes in. He comes up to the house. Nobody. He looks for the door, opens it and goes into rooms that are as cool and dark as cellars. Finally, he opens a small door and discovers a dark drawing-room where the Italian lady is seated. 'Come in,' she says. 'I was waiting for you.' She is eating figs and offers him some. She chats. She says that the house and grounds please her so much that she is thinking of buying it. She is a widow. She is young. She would like to meet a young man who loves the estate as she does and would help her to cultivate it and manage it. Under her bracelet she shows him an old tattoo, *Turbul*. She laughs. In short, she is charming, implying that the young man she is looking for is Georges. Georges makes his escape, pursued by her sardonic laughter. When he gets back to Peyrehorade, he begs his father to help him escape from an evil spell and to allow him to marry Julie. Admonished by Mme de Peyrehorade and Puygarrig, M. de Peyrehorade accepts. Engagement. The marriage is to take place on the 13th. Joy. The day before, on the morning of the 12th, Georges goes past Prades and cannot resist entering. He cannot open the gate. He walks round the estate, and talks to an old keeper. He asks if the lady is in. The servant, astonished, tells him that there is no one living in Prades, that his masters are travelling and have not let the place out to any lady. Georges loses his temper. The keeper thinks he is mad. He takes him up to the house and proves that everything is locked, the dust covers on, the shutters up and no one is living there.

Georges, appalled, rushes back to Peyrehorade where his father, his mother, Julie and the archaeologist are trying out the new stands and watching the locals playing tennis. He tears off his jacket and runs onto the court. He starts to play as if he was fighting. The family tries to calm him. He ignores them. He exhausts himself, playing on and on. He misses the ball. He gets angry. It is because of the ring he is wearing, which is getting in his way, a large ring composed of two joined hands which he wanted to give Julie as a wedding ring — (Julie found it too heavy and preferred a simple gold band). He takes the ring off, runs over to the Venus and puts it on her finger. Then he hurls himself back into the game, leaping, hitting and deliberately tiring himself out. They beg him to desist. No. He plays, plays, plays! He plays with such energy that he becomes faint. Julie runs forward. They take him back to the house almost senseless. The two old men exchange a silent glance. Mme de Peyrehorade weeps. Julie tends him. He sits up. 'Enough, I am not ill!' He bursts out laughing. 'Let's get ready for the feast.' A storm. It was the storm that was making him so tense! He hates it. A cloudburst. Suddenly, he remembers that he has left his ring on the Venus. Julie prevents him from going out. He can get the ring when the storm is over. She did not like that ring. She would be happy if he left it where it is and, tomorrow, put the plain little gold band on her finger.

The next day, a Friday (the Day of Venus, the archaeologist remarks), there is all the hustle and bustle of the wedding, with the carriages setting out for Perpignan. The Venus is forgotten. Sun. Dresses. Sunshades. New suits. Bouquets.

Perpignan. The wedding. The plain gold ring. As he puts it on his wife's finger, Georges remembers the ring he left behind at Peyrehorade and, during the mass, is obviously only thinking about that. The honeymoon is to take place in Peyrehorade. Joyful return. Georges is distant. He admits his worries to the archaeologist, who makes fun of him. The storm returns. They come back in the rain. A bolt of lightning falls not far from the shelter on the road where they are waiting for the rain to stop. At Peyrehorade, everyone dives into the house to change and get dry. Georges drinks a large glass of spirits and becomes slightly drunk. He is behaving more and more strangely. He sneaks out and goes to look for his ring in the pouring rain. The Venus. He reaches out his hand. But his face is contorted. The Venus has closed her fingers. He cannot get the ring off.

He rushes back towards the house, turning to look at the statue. He stumbles, falls over and is covered in mud. In this condition he appears before the family and, saying nothing to anyone, drags the archaeologist into the hall. He stutters. He is trembling. He grasps hold of Puygarrig who is very concerned at his state. Everyone is listening at the door, trying to hear what is being said. He tells Puygarrig about the fingers. Puygarrig thinks he is drunk. Georges wants to drag him outside. Puygarrig refuses and tries to persuade him that he is drunk and only imagined he saw the fingers locked together. He pulls him upstairs to his room. There, Georges lies sobbing, face down, telling a confused story about the ring and the empty house at Prades. He talks simultaneously of the Italian woman and the Venus. Puygarrig tries to calm him down and leaves him alone. He locks the door. He goes back down to the others and says it is nothing: Georges is over-excited with happiness and has drunk a little too much. Julie weeps. Mme de Peyrehorade consoles her. It's a celebration! Georges will rest. Julie should go up to the bridal chamber, go to bed and wait for him. She takes her to her room, helps her to undress, kisses her, hugs her and leaves her alone. The room is large, high-ceilinged, shaken by thunder and lightning. In the middle is a huge four-poster. Julie undoes her hair, paces around the room and kneels to pray. The parents ask Puygarrig to go up and see Georges, who is asleep. He wakes him up. Georges's terrified awakening. Puygarrig talks about his daughter and her love for him, lectures him and brings him back to real life. Georges is ashamed and promises Puygarrig that he will have no more attacks. He will make his daughter happy. He is not used to drink. He had been drinking!

It is night-time and the storm has worsened. 'Julie must be afraid, all by herself.' Georges must quickly go to their room and comfort her.

While they are talking, and almost laughing about their fears, they hear heavy footsteps coming up the stairs. They listen. 'It's Peyrehorade,' says the archaeologist. 'He is coming here. Calm down and don't say anything.' But the footsteps stop. 'He wants to know if everything is all right and if you have gone to join Julie.' Puygarrig opens the door and shouts: 'Georges was asleep. He is coming straight down. Go to bed and leave the lovers in peace.'

Georges goes down. Puygarrig looks after him, smiling, and shuts his door.

As the footsteps stopped, Julie, in the bedroom, having finished her prayers, had gone to bed, on the left-hand side, and with every flash of lightning hid her head under the clothes. Suddenly, she hears the footsteps approaching, sits up, dries her tears, pushes the hair back off her forehead, smiles and looks at the door. The door starts to open. She says: 'Georges, have you been drinking? Is that you? . . . ' The door opens. Her eyes widen, she stifles a scream and faints. At this moment we return to the threshold of the door where the archaeologist is encouraging Georges and looking after him.

Georges goes down the stairs and along the corridor. The curtains wave. The windows slam. He stops in front of the bridal chamber, knocks gently and goes in . . . He murmurs: 'Julie! . . . Do you forgive me? . . . '

M. and Mme Peyrehorade in their room. They cannot sleep. They are watching and waiting. Puygarrig, too, in his room. He paces up and down, puts out his lamp, relights it. Lightning strikes close by with a fearful din. The empty house, lit by flashes of lightning.

The door of the bridal chamber slowly opens onto the corridor. The Peyrehorades and Puygarrig are listening. At this point the camera does not follow the statue of Venus but the fearful traces that she leaves behind her. We hear every bronze footfall, only seeing the resulting devastation: broken stairs, balustrade torn out, ripped carpets, stair rods rolling, the paving stones in the hallway snapping, the front door hanging off its hinges, the footprints in the mud, the bench overturned and, finally, on her pedestal, the Venus, motionless. She slowly draws one foot under her robe.

The parents and the archaeologist have heard the din. They come out of their rooms in their nightclothes, holding lamps, and meet on the stairs. They ask what is happening. Was it the thunder? They see the broken staircase, the door hanging off. They follow the trail. The door of the bridal chamber is creaking, half-open. They call out. No answer. They dare not go in. The archaeologist calls again: 'Julie, Julie! Georges!' He tries to open the door, but the handle and lock fall to the ground. 'Julie, Julie!' He goes in. Peyrehorade follows him. 'Don't come in,' he shouts to his wife.

What they discover, the storm ended, in silence and

moonlight, is the scene of a crime. Julie is standing in a corner of the room, pointing, motionless, ashen. The hangings of the bed are down, the bedclothes disordered and, half hanging off the bed, his head back, Georges in the attitude of a man who has fallen from the fifth floor or been struck by lightning.

While Puygarrig rushes over to his daughter, who cannot see him, but looks in horror straight in front of her, Mme de Peyrehorade throws herself down like a madwoman beside the bed and tries to raise her son's head. Peyrhorade repeats: 'My God, my God!', trying to lift him by his shoulders and hands. At this point, Georges's hand releases the ring of Venus, which rolls across the floor. Julie's father is begging her to speak, to explain: she repeats in a toneless voice, almost a whisper, the one phrase: 'She hugged him, hugged him in her arms . . . She hugged him, hugged him in her arms . . . She hugged him, hugged him in her arms . . . '

Darkness, thunder.

We go back to the start of the film, on the road where Puygarrig is accompanying the doctor to his carriage. Tomorrow he will go to the hospital. 'There is the story . . . ' 'And,' the doctor asks, 'where is the statue?' 'M. and Mme Peyrehorade had it melted down and offered it to the church. That's the bell you can hear ringing this morning.' (Louder, funereal sound of the bell). 'I don't like the sound of that bell,' says the doctor. He takes the reins. The horse rears.

The black bell in full swing. Gathering clouds. Flight of birds away, calling. Peasants crossing themselves, shutting themselves in, looking at the harvest shaking their heads and mumbling: 'The Idol . . . The Idol . . . The Idol . . . It's the Idol . . . It's the Idol . . . It's the Idol . . . It's because of the Idol.' The camera shows the empty pedestal. The ghost of Georges has sat down on the bench and is playing *morra*, in the void, like a madman.

Bibliography

Translations of Jean Cocteau's own books include *Two Screenplays: the Blood of a Poet and The Testament of Orpheus* (tr. by C. Martin-Sperry, Marion Boyars, London, 1970), and two books published in Britain during Cocteau's lifetime, his *Diary of a Film: La Belle et la Bête* (tr. by R. Duncan, Dobson, London, 1950) and his conversations with André Fraigneau, *Cocteau on the Film* (tr. by V. Traill, Dobson, London, 1954). Arthur B. Evans examines a particular aspect of the work in *Jean Cocteau and His Films of Orphic Identity* (Art Alliance, 1978), and there is a chapter on the passage from novel to film in Robin Buss's study guide to *Cocteau: Les Enfants Terribles* (Grant and Cutler, London, 1986). Roy Armes's *French Cinema Since 1946: Vol. I: The Great Tradition* (Tantivy Press, London; A. S. Barnes, New York, 1966) has a section analyzing Cocteau among the 'veteran' directors of French cinema, beside Clair, Renoir, Carné and Ophuls.

Past Tense: The Cocteau Diaries (two vols., tr. by R. Howard, Harcourt Brace Jovanovich, New York, 1987, 1988) and *Cocteau's World: an Anthology of Writings* (ed. and tr. by M. Crosland, London, 1972) give a broader insight into the mind of a film-maker who was also a poet, novelist, playwright, artist and critic. Francis Steegmuller's *Cocteau* (Constable, London, 1970) is the standard biography in English, and there is an accessible illustrated life by A. K. Peters, *Jean Cocteau and His World* (Thames and Hudson, London, 1987).

Le Testament d'Orphée: *ph*. Roland Pontoizeau; *des*. Pierre Guffroy; *ed*. Marie-Josèphe Yoyotte; *mus*. Jacques Metehan; *prod*. Editions Cinématographiques; *with*: Jean Cocteau, Edouard Dermit, Henri Crémieux, Maria Casarès, François Périer, Yul Brynner, Jean-Pierre Léaud, Claudine Oger, Jean Marais. (1960)

16mm films directed by Cocteau

Coriolan (1950)

Villa Santo-Sospir (1952)

Films written or adapted by Cocteau

La Comédie du bonheur (1940; *d*. Marcel L'Herbier). Additional dialogues.

Le Baron fantôme (1943; *d*. Serge de Poligny). Adaptation and dialogues. Cocteau also played the part of Baron Carol.

L'Eternel retour (1943; *d*. Jean Delannoy). Screenplay and dialogues. Cocteau is sometimes also credited as co-director, and the film certainly shows evidence of his influence. It starred Jean Marais, Madeleine Sologne and Yvonne de Bray.

Les Dames du Bois de Boulogne (1945; *d*. Robert Bresson). Dialogues, and co-adaptor with Bresson, from a story by Diderot. Much as Cocteau admired Bresson, their styles were radically different.

Ruy Blas (1947; *d*. Pierre Billon). Dialogues and adaptation, from the play by Victor Hugo. Jean Marais starred, the music was by Georges Auric and art direction by Georges Wakhévitch.

Noces de Sable (1948; *d.* André Zwoboda). Commentary. The film is a version of the story of Tristan and Iseult, set in Morocco.

Les Enfants terribles (1950; *d.* Jean-Pierre Melville). Scenario, dialogues and adaptation, from his own novel (1929). An interesting attempt to film the novel, despite the difficulty of conveying its sexual undercurrents within the cinema conventions of the time.

La Princesse de Clèves (1960; *d.* Jean Delannoy). Dialogues and adaptation, from the novel by Mme de La Fayette. A rather unsuccessful attempt to film a classic novel, starring Jean Marais, with photography by Henri Alekan and music by Georges Auric.

Thomas l'imposteur (1965; *d.* Georges Franju). Dialogues and adaptation, from his own novel, set during the First World War (1923). Made after Cocteau's death, it had music by Georges Auric and the cast included Edouard Dermit.

Filmography

Commercial films directed by Cocteau

Le Sang d'un poète: *ph*. Georges Périnal; *des*. Jean d'Eaubonne; *mus*. Georges Auric; *prod*. Vicomte Charles A. de Noailles; *with*: Lee Miller, Pauline Carton, Odette Talazac, Enrique Rivero, Jean Desbordes. (1931)

La Belle et la Bête: *ph*. Henri Alekan; *art dir*. Christian Bérard; *des*. René Moulaert, Lucien Carré; *ed*. Claude Ibéria; *mus*. Georges Auric; *prod*. André Paulvé; *with*: Jean Marais, Josette Day, Mila Parély, Nane Germon, Michel Auclair, Marcel André. (1946)

L'Aigle à deux têtes: *ph*. Christian Matras; *art dir*. Christian Bérard; *des*. Georges Wakhévitch; *ed*. Claude Ibéria; *mus*. Georges Auric; *prod*. Ariane/Sirius; *with*: Jean Marais, Edwige Feuillère, Jean Debucourt, Sylvia Monfort, Jacques Varennes, Yvonne de Bray. (1947)

Les Parents terribles: *ph*. Michel Kelber; *art dir*. Christian Bérard; *des*. Guy de Gastyne; *ed*. Jacqueline Douarinou-Sadoul; *mus*. Georges Auric; *prod*. Ariane; *with*: Jean Marais, Josette Day, Yvonne de Bray, Marcel André, Gabrielle Dorziat. (1948)

Orphée: *ph*. Nicholas Hayer; *des*. Jean d'Eaubonne; *ed*. Jacqueline Douarinou-Sadoul; *mus*. Georges Auric; *prod*. André Paulvé/Les Films du Palais Royal; *with*: Jean Marais, Maria Casarès, François Périer, Marie Déa, Edouard Dermit, Juliette Gréco, Pierre Bertin, Jacques Varennes. (1950)

Index of proper names

Index of film titles